LOST 1
LESSONS
A DEVOTIONAL BY TEENS FOR TEENS

By
Dr. Randy T. Johnson
and
Dr. David Rutledge

RM Rochester Media

Published by:
Rochester Media LLC
P.O. Box 80002
Rochester, MI 48308
248-429-READ
www.rochestermedia.com

All scripture quotations, unless otherwise indicated, are taken from Holy Bible, New International Version NIV R (Reserved Symbol?) copyright C (Copyright Symbol?) 1973, 1978, 1984 by International Bible Society.

Author: Dr. Randy Johnson, David Rutledge
Cover Design & Formatting: Jamieson Design

First U.S. Edition Year 1st Edition was Published

Summary: Christian devotional based on the television series Lost ®

ISBN: 978-1499337068

1. Christian Living, Spiritual Growth, Christianity, Religion

For current information about releases by Dr. Randy Johnson or other releases from Rochester Media, visit our website: http://www.rochestermedia.com

Printed in the United States of America

Table of Contents

Preface

LOST Lessons was written by Randy Johnson and David Rutledge. The book is well received and is reaching varied individuals. Young adults who are dedicated followers of Jesus Christ are learning to see media, Hollywood and even the world from a Christian perspective, while those who are not necessarily connecting with a church are seeing Jesus in a fresh way. Based on this success, the authors decided to write on seasons 2-6 of *LOST*, but with a twist: they involved high school juniors and seniors. Those, too, are well received; so fifty-four students came together to rewrite season 1 from a teen perspective:

Angelica Allegro	Savannah Bell
Reuben Bettinger	Andrew Borja
Robert Borja	Madison Bottiaux
Andrew Bowling	Yue Yang "Ted" Chan
Zachary Clark	Daniel Cobb
Hannah Culver	Larissa Espinosa Perez
Francesca Golus	Adela Hajali
Spencer Haupert	Jennifer Hill
Marie Hoffman	Ashley Hoskins
Victoria Johns	James Kern
Soovin "Susan" Kim	Stuart Koppela-Sutherland
Jenna Kay Lamborn	Josiah Lasala
Dong "Jack" Lee	Shelby Lowe
Emily Lowell	Brandon Lucas

Austin Miller
Mary Katherine Morgan
Anna Mullaly
Katie Piot
Robert Roose
Daniel G. Smith
Hannah Snyder
Chase Sumner
Tianquan "Summer" Wang
Lauren Wisnoski
Sara Wright

Sara Wright
Rachel Mueller
Stephen Nichols
Michelle Roldan
Jason Schomer
Daniel W. Smith
Daniel Stockton
John Van Noord
Kathryn Willson
Chyenne Witt

Graphics Team:

Bethany Garcia - Captain
Elaine Haggard
Cassidy Okonsk
Laura Morse
Kristen Eckhout i

LOST Lessons is designed as a "devotional by teens, for teens." This group of fifty-four students at Oakland Christian School broke into small groups, watched an episode of *LOST*, discussed the spiritual implications and then wrote a devotion. Randy Johnson and David Rutledge gave direction and modified the lessons, striving to ensure good Biblical support and a flow that is easier to read. Each lesson begins with a pretty extensive overview of the episode, so someone who has not watched the show can still benefit from the devotional.

Randy Johnson and David Rutledge would like to say a special thank you to Tom Gendich and Rochester Media for believing in youth and publishing *LOST Lessons*, and a thank you to the other professionals who helped:

Laura Hall (http://rebornagain2010.wordpress.com/about-me/) edited the lessons for clarity, spelling and grammar.

Brian Jamieson (http://www.jamiesondesign.net) designed the cover and the book layout.

Chapter 1

■ ■ ■

Slingshot

Episode 1
Pilot (Part 1)

Flight 815 has crashed onto an uncharted island. Jack, one of the passengers on the plane, wakes up bewildered in the jungle. The plane has been split into two, leaving people in disarray. No one knows what has happened or what to do next. The passengers of the plane don't know who to turn to for guidance. Jack realizes that there is no one else on the island who will step up to be a leader, and that he must take on the role of leadership if he wants the stranded to survive. Jack steps up to the plate by helping to heal people by using his skills as a doctor to help the injured people.

"He sounds like a very smart man."

Jack takes control by helping revive a dead woman named Rose. Napoleon Bonaparte says, "A leader is a dealer in hope."

Part of being a good leader is being aware of ones surroundings. Jack sees the hanging wing of the wrecked plane about to fall and takes initiative by rescuing a lady who is in danger. As a leader one has to take risks. Jack demonstrates this by taking Kate and Charlie into the jungle, in search of the missing cockpit. Even though this means separating from the group and going into danger. Jack puts himself last and is always thinking of the others. Jack also gives up his sleep in order to treat every that's in need of medical attention.

In the Bible, God appoints us to be leaders. A perfect example of this is David and Goliath. In 1 Samuel 17:1 God has the Israelite's in a tough position. The Philistines are threating to destroy them unless they can over come their best warrior Goliath, a nine-foot giant.

God gave the Israelites David to be a leader in tough times. David wasn't told ahead of time and was not anything special he just responded to God's call

He will protect him in battle.

There was a lot of pressure for David to win this battle. If he lost, the whole nation of Israel would become enslaved to the Philistines. He did not make excuses to God about how he could not fight Goliath, or that the pressure was too great. He accepted that God was using him to save his nation, and had faith that God would take care of him.

Although he is young in age, he had courage through God. David was the youngest in his family; no one expected anything out of him. The only role in life to this point in time is to take care of the sheep. It was the role of his brothers to be warriors and soldiers of the Israelite army. Instead David stepped up and faced his people's enemy single-handed.

As Christians we are designed to be leaders in our communities. We are the sons and daughters of the Creator, and although we are not armed with a sword or a slingshot, we do have the faith courage and protection 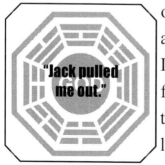 of God. The Bible states that we are supposed to be God's light. In Matthew 5:14 Jesus tells His followers, "You are the light of the world." We are called to be leaders in the world by showing and stepped up to fight Goliath. Ray Croc says, "The quality of a leader is reflected in the standard they set for themselves." You don't have to be anything special to do God's work. You just have to be willing to step up and accept the challenge He is giving to you.

David did not use any special armor to defeat Goliath. He used the resources he already had to defeat him. He used stones and a slingshot to defeat Goliath, not fancy armor that other soldiers had. He was a simple boy, which was reflected in his simple weapons. God does not need anything or anyone special to do His work with; He often works through the common person. Goliath in comparison had the most advanced amour. 1 Samuel 17:5-7says, "He had a helmet

"[About plane turbulence] It's normal."

of bronze on his head, and he was armed with a coat of mail, and the weight of the coat was five thousand shekels of bronze. And he had bronze armor on his legs, and a javelin of bronze slung between his shoulders. The shaft of his spear was like a weaver's beam, and his spear's head weighed six hundred shekels of iron." David was given a helmet and chain mail to fight Goliath, but choose to have faith in God, and trust that them the light of God. In Psalms 36:9 it says, "For with you is the fountain of life; in your light we see light."

Christ is the ultimate example of light to us. He healed the blind and casted out demons. As Christians we are supposed to try and be like Christ and follow His example. He walked into dark areas of the world and filled them with light. John 1:5 tells us "The light shines in the darkness; and the darkness did not comprehend it."

It takes courage and trust in God to be able to try and share Christ light in dark areas. Schools, the workplace and bars are perfect examples of dark places that the ordinary Christian can be a light to. Hebrews 10:35 says, "So don't lose the courage that you had in the past. Your courage will be rewarded richly." We should be like Jack who showed no sign of fear, and intrigued Kate enough to ask, "You don't seem afraid at all. I don't understand." Christians should be able to encourage others in the same way. If a child of God is weak at heart and afraid, but then sees a fellow Christian who is unafraid it will build the weak one up. If there are Christians in foreign countries willing to die to so they can spread the words of Christ we should be unafraid to do the same when are only punishment is the possibility of being mocked.

Do you think God has a leadership role for you?

_____

_____

_____

_____

What do you think is holding you back?

_____

_____

_____

_____

What do you think God has equipped you with?

_____

_____

_____

_____

How can we be a light to others?

_____

_____

_____

_____

"A leader is one who knows the way, goes the way, and shows the way."
– John C. Maxwell

Chapter 2

■ ■ ■

One Tangible Contribution

Episode 2
Pilot (Part 2)

While looking for the other parts of the plane, Jack, Charlie, and Kate find the front half, along with the pilot who is still alive. After relaying to the pilot what has happened, the four hear the mysterious monster approaching. As the pilot tries to use the transceiver to contact help, the scene becomes completely silent. Within seconds the pilot is grabbed by the monster and is quickly killed. Jack, Charlie, and Kate run for their lives. In fear, Kate runs and doesn't look back. Charlie trips, falls, and is stuck in part of the

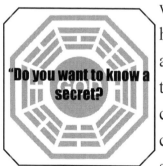
"Do you want to know a secret?"

ground. His fear prevents him from escaping. Luckily, Jack notices Charlie is missing and runs to save him. Jack steps in the place of both of their fear and takes them to safety away from the monster. When we are afraid, we want someone to step in to save us, just like Jack did for Charlie.

Like Jack saved Charlie, in the Bible, Aaron saved Moses in the face of fear. The Lord called Moses to free the Israelites from slavery in Egypt. Knowing that he would go through many hardships freeing the Israelites, Moses was afraid of leading by himself. His major fear - public speaking - was holding him

back from doing what God instructed him to do. He did not feel adequate enough to be the speaker for the people of Israel. In Exodus 4 Moses asks, "What if they do not believe me or listen to me and say, 'The Lord did not appear to you?'" The Lord immediately answered Moses' questions through the extraordinary. First, The Lord turned Moses' staff into a snake. With the touch of his hand and by the power of God, Moses turned the snake back into a staff. Second, the Lord told Moses to put his hand in his cloak and then take it out again. When he did this, his hand was covered with leprosy. After Moses took his hand out of his cloak a second time, his hand was restored and God's power was shown.

Even after what Moses just saw, he was still doubtful of God's command. When Moses expressed his feelings of fear to the Lord, the Lord became furious because of Moses' lack of faith. Who was Moses to tell God whether he was able to take on the task or not? You see, God knew all of Moses' fears and was willing to assist him. All that Moses had to do was believe. Even though Moses doubted, the Lord sent Aaron, Moses' brother, to speak in place of Moses. Moses and Aaron went to Egypt together to free the Israelites. With Moses speaking the words of the Lord through Aaron,

they did great things and were able to free the Israelites. Rainer Maria Rilke has said, "One had to take some action against fear when it laid hold of one." Just as Aaron takes the place of Moses in his fear of speaking, God was able to present this opportunity for someone to step in the place of another's fear.

Name a time when someone has contributed something or in some way contributed to helping you, whether you were afraid or in need of help.

_____

_____

_____

_____

Name a time when you have helped someone else by contributing in some way for them when they afraid or needed help.

_____

_____

_____

_____

Walter Annenberg states, "You will not be satisfied unless you are contributing something to or for the benefit of others." When we step in the place of someone else's fear, it allows us to show God's love and the way that He cares for us. By contributing in our fear or in place of others' fear, we are like Jack. Jack stepped in to save Charlie's life when they both were in a dire situation. Likewise, in Isaiah 41:13, the Lord says, "For I am the Lord your God who takes hold of your right hand and says to you, Do not fear; I will help you." He is always with us and will provide ways for us to contribute and praise Him in our fear.

How has helping someone, or someone else's contributions to you been benefiting

_____

_____

_____

_____

What are 5 ways people around the world continue to contribute to others? What about when they are fearful and need help?

_____

_____

_____

_____

What would our world be like if no one stepped in and contributed to others, especially if they are fearful?

_____

_____

_____

_____

Like Charlie, we all want someone to save us, especially when we have fear, but in our fear we can do something else. We can contribute. In Jack's fear for his life, he goes back and saves Charlie's life. Similarly, Aaron speaks for Moses to the Pharaoh when he is afraid. Think of the things you wrote down with the questions above. How has someone stepped in for you when you were afraid? How did that situation affect you? Each and every day God steps in for us when we are fearful. He is an active part of our lives whether we know it or not. Romans 8:31 tells us that if God is on

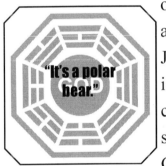

our side, then no one can come against us. Just like Charlie, Jack, Kate, and everyone on the island is fearful, they also must come together and contribute something in order to survive. God sent his son, Jesus, to die for us. In Jesus' reservations and not wanting to die a painful death on the cross, He did it. He stepped in for us and paid the price for all of our sins so that we can be blameless in God's eyes. For every trek, there is one tangible contribution.

In Acts 7:22 it is said, "Moses was educated in all the wisdom of the Egyptians and was powerful in speech and action." Moses had everything going for him and all was set in place for him to accomplish what God commanded. He grew up in the Egyptian palace where people catered to his needs and gave him a great education. Out of all people in Egypt, God chose one of the most able people. Moses was educated, able, and now he must be willing. Through this example of Moses, we can see that most times, when God asks something of you, He is asking something of you that you can conquer and meet his expectations. Too many of us today are put into situations where we hide in our fear and doubt our abilities. In these types of situations, look to God. He is purposely placing you in a situation that, with Him, you can handle. As you go throughout the next few days, intentionally think of the situations you are in now. Are you fearful? Can God use you in your fear? Even though you have fear, are you able?

"The only thing to fear is fear itself"
– Franklin D. Roosevelt

Chapter 3

■ ■ ■

Redemptive Liberation

Episode 3
"Tabula Rasa"

In episode three of season one, Jack continues to try and save a man's life that is slowly dying from the shrapnel that is lodged into his chest. In the midst of Jack's last efforts, the man who he is trying to save, a U.S. Marshall, constantly murmurs, "don't trust her," and  "she's dangerous." While trying to figure out who the Marshall is talking about, Jack finds a picture of Kate's mug shot in his pocket.

Meanwhile, the people who climb inland to gain higher land to try and call for help with the receiver are on their way back to the beach, but decide to make camp in a clearing to avoid traveling in the jungle at night. During the campfire, Sayid convinces the group that they should keep the French woman's message to themselves, because if they were to tell the others they would lose hope, and they cannot afford to loose hope.

Later on, when Hurly finds Kate's mug shot, he immediately asks Jack if he knows what she did. Jack responds by saying that he doesn't know what she did, but at this point it doesn't matter, and it's none of their business.

Finally, Kate flashes back to when she was held at gunpoint by a farmer, on his farm for sleeping in his barn. After talking things over, they both realize they can help each other. Kate could use the lodging and the pay, and the farmer needs work to be done around the farm.

Ludwig Wittgenstein once said, "A confession has to be part of your new life." Kate tries to tell Jack what she did. Jack tells Kate that their past lives aren't important anymore saying, "We all died when we came to the Island." This relates to a story in the Bible of the woman at the well. This story took place in

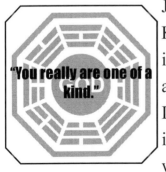

"You really are one of a kind."

a time when Jews and Samaritans did not get along. The main reason that they did not get along was due to biblical disagreements. The Samaritans rejected some parts of the Old Testament, and this offended the Jews. Jews considered Samaritans to be lower-class citizens. The hatred between these two people groups went so far, that if a Jew wanted to draw water from a well, they would not go if a Samaritan was there. Jesus, however, did not differentiate. Jesus knew that the woman was a Samaritan, yet he still went to the well.

In John 4:9-10, it says, "The Samaritan woman said to him, 'I am a Samaritan and you are a Jew, how is it that you ask me for a drink?' And Jesus answered her, 'if you knew the gift of God, and he that asks you for a drink you would have asked him and he would have given you living water.'" Jesus also doesn't care

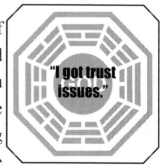

that she "got around" or the fact that she already had five husbands and was with another man who is not her husband. Even with her socially unacceptable lifestyle and her heritage, Jesus still offers her the water of eternal life. Jesus offers this to her freely. He would die to pay the penalty for sin and He doesn't worry about what we have done because He loves us all. Jesus doesn't care about all the things she has done in her life if she accepts His offer of eternal life. With this renewal, she will have a completely new life and her old life will have "died." This idea is also expressed in 2 Corinthians 5:17, "Therefore, if anyone is in Christ, the new creation has come: The old has gone, the new is here!" God offers a fresh start.

Similarly, in LOST, when they crashed on the Island, their old lives didn't matter anymore. 1 John 1:9 says, "If we confess our sins, he is faithful and just to forgive us our sins and to cleanse us from all unrighteousness." It doesn't matter what any of them did or said in their old lives, they have all turned over a new leaf and they must help each other and try to survive. Isaiah 43:18 says, "Remember not the former things, nor consider the things of old."

Kate must have felt like William Green when he quoted, "I feel like I have a new life and I'm going to take full advantage of it." Jack shows characteristics of Christ when he tells Kate he doesn't want to know what she did. Romans 5:8 says, "But God shows his love for us in that while we were still sinners, Christ died for us." Everyone else seems to be so concerned with finding out what Kate did, but not Jack. His maturity shows in this

"Don't trust her. She's dangerous."

episode because he knows that whatever Kate did is irrelevant. A second chance is a powerful, life-changing thing to be given. As Lance Armstrong said, "If you ever get a second chance for something, you've got to go all the way." Because Kate was given this opportunity, she must take full advantage of it. Everyone is equal on the Island; Kate must start a brand new life much like the woman at the well.

What do you struggle with the most?

_____

_____

_____

_____

Do you feel afraid to come to God because of your shortcomings?

_____

_____

_____

_____

Are you afraid of judgment, not only by God, but peers for what you have done?

_____

_____

_____

_____

Do you try to cover up the past?

_____

_____

_____

_____

Have you moved on from the past? – If not, what is stopping you?

_____

_____

_____

_____

"We all have big changes in our lives that are more or less a second chance."

- Harrison Ford

Chapter 4

■ ■ ■

Suffering: Being Jesus to Others

Episode 4
"Walkabout"

In episode four, the survivors from the crash are dealing with the loss of life and injuries caused by the accident and people are dealing with the situation differently. The majority of the people are trying to focus on surviving, while others are barely able to cope with the trauma they have just experienced. An example of a person having to deal with suffering is Rose. She is completely overcome with sadness because of the death of her husband. She separates herself from the rest

of the group and mourns his death in silence. Boone is the first one to notice Rose sitting alone. He asks who should be the one to go check on her, in response, his sister Shannon laughs at him and says, "I nominate you Captain America." This is an example of how people deal with stress and those who are suffering around them. Some people, like Boone, notice and become sympathetic towards the suffering, but do not act on their feeling of a need to do something. Some, like Shannon, shut down and become more concerned with their own problems, but some people, like Jack, are forced into action, not because they want to but because they feel a moral obligation to react and help those who are in need. When Jack comes to comfort her, she does not talk to him for quite some time. She refuses

"You have to get into the mind of the fish."

to take care of herself, and just stares out to the sea, twiddling her husband's wedding ring that she wore on her necklace. Although she did not respond to Jack immediately, his presence alone was comforting to Rose, and she eventually talks to him. The only reason she comes back to the people and takes care of herself is because she has faith that her husband is still alive somewhere.

Everyone goes through a time of pain and struggle. Helen Keller states, "Character cannot be developed in ease and quiet. Only through experience of trial and suffering can the soul be strengthened, ambition inspired, and success achieved." In times of suffering, many people seclude themselves from their friends and loved ones because they do not want to be pitied or a burden to anyone. As Christians, it is our job to be Jesus to others, and help find the lost and carry the weak back to His presence. Sometimes, all that people need is to know there is a person, in their presence, who genuinely cares for them and wants to help them. It does not necessarily mean they want to stop what they are doing or listen to what that person is saying, but the mere action of coming to the suffering person's aid can drastically change the person's outlook on the situation.

""Wherever they are now- they are not alone."

In Matthew 18, Jesus says to his disciples, "Again, truly I tell you that if two of you on earth agree about anything they ask for, it will be done for them by my Father in heaven. For where two or three gather in my name, there am I with them." This means that if we see someone suffering, we should pray for them, and come in the presence of believers and make them aware of the situation, so they may gather and pray as well. If the Spirit is tugging on your heart to comfort someone in need, then the first step is prayer (Matt. 18:19-20).

However, we are not just called to be people of prayer but of action. There is a place for prayer and it is very powerful, but if our prayers do not become actions, then they are somewhat empty. Walter Anderson says, "I can choose to sit in perpetual sadness, immobilized by the gravity of my loss, or I can choose to rise from the pain and treasure the most precious gift I have- life itself." Jack rose from the accident and did not allow it to shake him. He was aware of his surroundings, and not caught up in himself. In Galatians 6:1-2 when Paul is addressing the church he says, "Brothers and sisters, if someone is caught in a sin, you who live by the Spirit should restore that person gently. But watch yourselves, or you also may be tempted. Carry each other's burdens, and in this way you will fulfill the law of Christ." This means that if we see people suffering, whether they are a Christians or not, we should be with them and help them carry their burdens. This could mean that we must tell them gently what they are doing wrong or help them with a task that they have been struggling with in their lives. Whatever the case, in order to truly help carry a person's burdens with them, they must pray continuously, and know that only through God's strength they can be renewed.

A perfect example of being there to comfort those who are suffering and helping carry their burdens with them is in John 11. Jesus' friend Lazarus was passing away from sickness. Jesus decides to go be with and comfort the two women who were with Lazarus. When Jesus arrived from the three-day trip, Lazarus had already passed away. The two women ask why He did not come earlier, because if He did, they knew Lazarus would not have died. Jesus becomes sympathetic of the two women and begins to weep with them, because He knew the pain and anguish they both were in. He felt the pain of the family who just lost their loved one, and comforted them with His mere presence. His way of helping carry the burden for the women and family was to raise Lazarus from the dead!

In our busy lives, it is sometimes easy to get caught up in daily activities, and not pay attention to those around us. On the island, Jack was driving himself mad because of all the different tasks he had to do and all the people who were relying on him. Although all of this chaos in his life was going on, Jack took time out of his busy life to go comfort an old lady, by just sitting with her. Not many words were spoken, but his mere action of sitting by her and telling her he would keep his promise, was exactly what Rose needed. When we feel a tugging on our heart to go be with someone and comfort them, whether they be a friend or not, we cannot shy away from that calling. Our response should be to pray for God's blessing and His guidance, then become people of action, doing what God calls us to do.

Have you ever had a devastating loss in your life?

_____

_____

_____

_____

Has someone every come beside you when you were down? How did it help?

_____

_____

_____

_____

Have you ever come beside someone during a time of grief?

_____

_____

_____

_____

In John 11 Jesus tells us to carry each other's burdens, how can you help someone you know carry a burden they are struggling with?

_____

_____

_____

_____

"No man is an island""
– John Donne

Chapter 5

■ ■ ■

Faith in You Means Faith in Him

Episode 5
"White Rabbit"

Up to this point, Lost has promoted the idea of strength. After all, it takes extreme mental strength to recover from such a horrid and unexpected accident like a plane crash. We see the leaders of the pack start to rise up. Jack, being a doctor, has been nominated to be the main one in charge of the stranded passengers: something he believes he is not ready for. The obvious spiritual application here is "Do you have what it takes?" Well, of course you do, as long as you recognize God is in power. However, we

"Crazy people don't know they are going crazy"

wanted to take a slightly different angle on that topic. Instead of focusing on getting through trials by trusting in God, we wanted to talk more about the need for inner strength during those trials.

It is important to have strength. Every Biblical character there is shows that. However, it is one of the topics that people try to avoid, because it is an easy concept to grasp. It is easy to talk about, but hard to actually do. As Christians, we need to understand ourselves. We are all specially designed by God with individual strengths and weaknesses. If we take the time

"Who packs 400 knives?"

to understand what is going on with us, we can get a better understanding of God's will for us. As promoters of the Word, we must be ready to face hardship, but if we doubt our ability to carry out God's Will, it will never get done. Sometimes God asks us to do something that may be out of our comfort zone. As followers, we should be prepared and willing to do whatever is needed and whenever it is asked- even if it seems too different. "The worst enemy to creativity is self-doubt," says Sylvia Plath. We can apply this concept with our mission of spreading The Gospel. Sometimes life calls for a little creativity in order to get the job done. However, when we doubt ourselves, we doubt in Him; for it is He who has made us, and He who gives us what we need to succeed. All we have to do is have faith in our abilities, given to us by the Lord.

Jack is going through a rough time. All his life he was told how he was just not meant to succeed, it just wasn't an option. That quickly took a toll on his mental strength, and he started to doubt his abilities. When faced with the thirst and hunger of all the people on the island, somebody had to step up to the plate, and of

"You are in my light, sticks."

course; Jack was the best possible choice. However, we see Jack's reaction as that of anger and hatred. This can all be linked back to the mental destruction he allowed to happen in years past. Joseph Addison once said, "He who hesitates is lost. Swift and resolute action leads to success. Self-doubt is a prelude to disaster." Had Jack taken a brief moment to chat with the Lord, discuss what is going on, and try to make it better, episode 5 might have looked a little different. Instead, Jack's mental health starts to diminish because the stress of being a leader is overwhelming, and he is wasting time pondering if he has the skill to lead that group of people.

This situation is similar to the story in Matthew chapter 14, where Peter was walking on the water with Jesus. While in a fishing boat, Peter and the other disciples saw Jesus walking out to them on the water. When Jesus called out for Peter to walk out and join Him, he had faith in Jesus and got out of the boat. However, Peter started to doubt the minute he started focusing on the storm. That is when he lost focus on Jesus, Himself, and he started to sink. Peter called out for Jesus to save him and when He did, Jesus asked him why he doubted. This is a perfect example of why we need to have confidence as Christians. Samuel Johnson stated, "Self-confidence is the first requisite to great undertakings." Though Johnson was not known as a prominent religious figure, this is exactly what the Bible teaches us.

Just to be clear, this is not promoting self-pride. God has given us everything, so we are not the ones who should be taking credit for our abilities/talents. This also does not mean that we only need to trust ourselves in times of trouble. By trusting in ourselves, we trust in God. It is just another way of looking at it.

Another example of this topic is found in 2 Corinthians chapter 3. "Such confidence we have through Christ before God. Not that we are competent in ourselves to claim anything for ourselves, but our competence comes from God. He has made us competent as ministers of a new covenant – not of the letter

"We worked it out caveman style."

but of the Spirit; for the letter kills, but the Spirit gives life" (Verses 4-6). Paul is talking to the Church of Corinth, and he is asking them to "toughen up." During this time, Christianity was not popular, and those in the Church were hesitant to spread His Word. Their own self-doubt hindered them from promoting and saving others. In a way, this mind-set can be equated to selfishness. God gives us competence, so we can have confidence in our abilities

As previously stated, our confidence can only be through the Lord. Once we fully embrace it, we are unstoppable. Also, this confidence is to be used at all times, but with discretion. Have no fear of expressing the Spirit of the Lord, but do not boast of accomplishments you carried out for Him because that defeats His entire purpose.

Philippians 4:13, "I can do all this through Him who gives me strength" is one of the most common verses known to Christians. It is the cookie-cutter, Sunday-school type verse, but it has such a deep meaning. We can and we will do all the things God has planned for us, and we know this is possible because we have the strength of the Lord. Who shall we fear?

What are some weaknesses you think you have?

_____

_____

_____

_____

What do you need to do to strengthen those weaknesses?

_____

_____

_____

_____

Were you ever required to be a leader? Did you step up to the plate?

_____

_____

_____

_____

When was the last time you doubted yourself/your abilities? Why?

_____

_____

_____

_____

How can you promote this "self-confidence in Christ" concept to others?

_____

_____

_____

_____

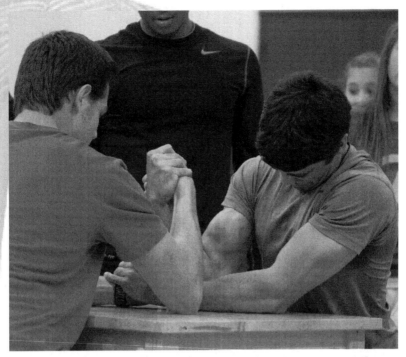

"Physical strength is measured by what we carry. Inner strength is measured by what we can bear."

– Anonymous

Chapter 6

■ ■ ■

Choose to Choose

Episode 6
"House of the Rising Sun"

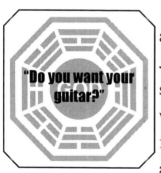

In Episode 6 we learn more about Sun and Jin. We saw how Jin proposed to Sun. We also saw how their marriage got worse when Jin decided to work for Sun's Father. We are shown a series of flashbacks that tell us that Sun wanted out of their marriage. During the scene where Jin attacks Michael we start to see Jin's temper. Sawyer and Sayid rush in to pull Jin off of Michael and lock Jin up until the whole thing can be sorted out.

Kate, Jack, Charlie and Locke go out in search of water and supplies from the plane wreckage. Charlie steps on a beehive and sends them all running. In the chaos, Jack and Kate come across caves that have fresh water. Kate and Jack go into the caves to get water and end up finding 2 bodies and name them "our very own Adam and Eve." Jack decides it would be easier to take the people to the caves to get water than it would be to try to take enough water to the people. The people then have to make a decision whether to stay at the beach and be visible for rescue or move to the caves by the water and shelter.

In the meantime, Locke helps Charlie to make the decision between his drug addictions and his guitar. In Deuteronomy 30:19 it says, "…Now you choose life, so that you and your children may live." This applies to Charlie because he made the choice to give up heroin. Sun approaches Michael on her husband's behalf to try to make him understand why he was attacked. Michael  had assumed it was because he was black. We find out that Sun speaks English and she decides to talk to Michael even though her husband did not know. She reveals that Jin was defending her family honor and trying to get her father's watch back. Sun asks Michael for a favor to free Jin and to give the watch back.

The survivors had a decision to make: stay at the beach or go to the caves. Each person had their own reasoning behind it because of what they have been through in their lifetime. Roy Disney said, "It's not hard to make decisions when you know what your values are." Each person has their own values in which influence their choices on where they wanted to stay, or even in Charlie's case whether he wanted to give up heroin for his guitar. In John 8:47 it says, "Whoever is of God hears the words of God. The reason why you do not hear them is that you are not of God." This scripture says that if you do not hear God it is because you are not of God. In order to be of God you must listen to what He wants for your life.

"Are you sure this is where you want to be?"

We can relate our lives to this because we make choices that we think will work out in our favor. In reality, we really should be making choices in the way God wants us to. Throughout this episode many decisions are made, most of which are made for personal decisions rather than what is best for the group. If you follow God's path, He will help lead you to where you need to be. Cassandra Clare in the City of Glass says,

"In the end that was the choice you made and it doesn't matter how hard it was to make it. It matters that you did."

The story of Adam and Eve, begins when God creates them in His own image. He puts them in a beautiful garden where He knows they will have everything they need. Among this garden are many trees and plants, including the Tree of Life and the Tree of Knowledge of Good and Evil. The Tree of Life had the power 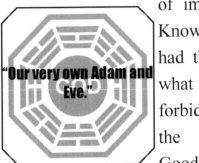 of immortality and the Tree of Knowledge of Good and Evil had the power to show them "Our very own Adam and Eve." what was right and wrong. God forbids them from eating from the Tree of Knowledge of Good and Evil. Yet, they were given the power to choose. Eventually both Adam and Eve go against the command. Genesis 3:6 says, "When the woman saw that the fruit was good for food and pleasuring to the eye, and also desirable for gaining wisdom, she took some and ate it. She also gave her husband who was with her, and he ate it."

This applies to our daily lives because a lot of the time we make choices knowing we shouldn't. We also make choices knowing that God doesn't want us to make them. As said by Sean Paul Sartre, "We are our choices." The choices that we make show a lot about who we are as individuals and as Christians. We need to make our choices according to what God wants for us and what is best for our life with Him.

When was a time in the past when you made a bad decision?

_____

_____

_____

_____

When was a time when you made a tough but right decision?

_____

_____

_____

_____

What decision are you wrestling with right now?

_____

_____

_____

_____

Are you willing to do the right thing even if it is difficult?

_____

_____

_____

_____

"It's our choices that show what we truly are, far
more than our abilities"-
– J.K. Rowling

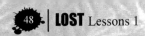

Chapter 7

■ ■ ■

From Heroin to Hero

Episode 7
"The Moth"

In episode seven, Charlie has flashbacks of his life as a rock star and all the mistakes he has made. He has just finished with confession at his church, when he sees his older brother, Liam, waiting for him in the church pews. Liam wants Charlie to join the band again, but Charlie is hesitant because he knew all the temptations he would face traveling with the band. Charlie makes his brother promise they both will quit the band if it gets too wild and out of control, Liam agrees. Over time, Charlie becomes increasingly agitated with his brother's antics. He would sing Charlie's parts of songs, hog all the attention, drink too much alcohol, have sex with girls in his dressing room, and, eventually, he began doing heroin. Years later, Charlie visits Liam and asks if he will join the band again for their comeback tour. Liam refuses and becomes angry with Charlie for still using drugs. Charlie tells Liam it is his fault that he was addicted to the drugs and angrily leaves Liam's house to catch a plane.

In this episode, Charlie is faced with many difficulties. On the Island, the heroin supply is limited; he attempts to stop his addiction. Locke helps him in the process by holding it for him and forcing him to ask three times for the drug. In the end of this episode, a cave crashes in on Jack and Charlie. Charlie is able to escape, but Jack is trapped. As the group of people frantically dig, Charlie volunteers to squeeze through a small hole in order to be by Jack again. Charlie ends up rescuing Jack, and turns from an outcast to a hero amongst the survivors. Throughout episode seven, Charlie develops and matures as a person. He learns that it is important to take responsibility for your actions.

God encourages His children to take responsibility for who they are and what they do. Solomon states in Ecclesiastes 11:9, "You who are young, be happy while you are young, and let your heart give you joy in the days of your

"Bless me father for I have sinned."

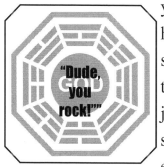
"Dude, you rock!'"

youth. Follow the ways of your heart and whatever your eyes see, but know that for all these things God will bring you into judgment." This means that we should enjoy our youthfulness, energy, and freedom that have been given to us from our Creator, but know that we are not invincible. One glorious day, each one of us will meet with God and have to take responsibility for our lives. It is not about finding a safe balance between fun and God; it's about glorifying God and through all aspects of life. In LOST, Charlie wants to live the wild life as a young man. He has a rude awakening when that option is taken away from him. As teens or young adults, it is easy to wish you could live the fast life. It seems riveting and new. God wants us to live a happy and exciting life, but He wants us to glorify Him in everything we do. Are you on the path for a rude awakening?

As Locke helped Charlie grow and mature, Christ-followers are called to help each other grow and mature in their spiritual walk. No matter how many other people you have helping and supporting you, eventually, you will need to take responsibility.

Locke forces Charlie to ask for the drugs three times. Charlie was forced to choose his path. Patrick Ness illustrates Locke's reasoning behind his test in this quote, "To say you have no choice is to relieve yourself of responsibility." When you claim you have to do something, you disown responsibility. We come to a point in life where we can grow from our mistakes, or hide under our rock, pretending nothing ever happened.

We learn from Charlie that when we admit our mistakes, we find peace. This does not mean it will be easy, but it will be a weight lifted off your shoulder. When Charlie professes the news of his addiction to Jack, Jack uses his wisdom in the medical field to encourage him. Proverbs 23:13 states, "Whoever conceals their sins does not prosper, but the one who confesses and renounces them finds mercy." By simply admitting that we are wrong in a situation, we humbly open ourselves up to correction. We cannot become stronger people of God unless we work through our struggles, as hard as that may be. It is incredibly hard laying down our pride, but necessary in order to develop into the men and women God created us to be.

In the caves, Jack confronted Charlie about his drug use and tells him to rest from the pains of withdrawal. Charlie becomes so infuriated with his suggestion that he yelled at Jack; causing a cave-in. Charlie ends up rescuing Jack and turns from an outcast to a hero amongst the survivors. Charlie decides to end his temptations once and for all. He asks Locke for his drugs the third time then proceeds to throw them in the fire. The passage in Matthew, "If your hand or your foot causes you to stumble, cut it off and throw it away. It is better  for you to enter life maimed or crippled than to have two hands or two feet and be thrown into eternal fire" (Matthew 18:8), best explains why Charlie threw his drugs away. He realizes if he never got rid of them, that they would be a constant distraction for him. Charlie was strengthened by the test Locke gave him and was able to break free from his bondage of drugs. Confucius boldly says, "Attack the evil that is within yourself, rather than attacking the evil that is in others." We get angry with others, when it is really us who are causing the problems. Taking responsibility for our mistakes is incredibly important.

To conclude, in life and as Christ-followers, there will always be different struggles and temptations. All people are sinners and are constantly battling to

"I wouldn't have taken you for a religious man."

do what is right. As stated in Corinthians, "No temptation has overtaken you except what is common to mankind. And God is faithful; he will not let you be tempted beyond what you can bear. But when you are tempted, he will also provide a way out so that you can endure it" (1 Corinthians 10:13). God allows us to be tempted in order to strengthen and prepare us for the hardships we will have to endure. We will be strengthened by doing what He has called us to do, and by spreading His Word to those who need it. Locke allows Charlie to suffer and be tempted in order to strengthen and prepare him for different hardships he would face on the island. Charlie decided, on his own, that he would throw away his drugs in order to better himself and the entire group on the island. God can use every struggle and hardship that we will face in our lives for good. While we need to take responsibility for our actions, it is also important to understand that we are completely and totally forgiven from our sins of the past if we have chosen to welcome God into our lives. He loves us so much that he sent his only Son for us, using Him as a perfect sacrifice, to bring us sinners back to Him. If we have chosen to accept Him into our lives, our past is erased in His eyes. Yes, we will need to deal with the worldly consequences, but by God's incredible grace, we have freedom to be with Him for eternity.

In what area are you taking responsibility in your life?

_____

_____

_____

_____

Is there an area that you know you need to take responsibility for, but are afraid to do anything about?

_____

_____

_____

Do you have godly friends who will challenge you to take credit for your actions?

_____

_____

_____

_____

Does your relationship with Jesus Christ give you a sense of peace?

_____

_____

_____

_____

"If you could kick the person in the pants responsible for most of your trouble, you wouldn't sit for a month."

– Mortimer Adler

Chapter 8

■ ■ ■

Emerging into my Enemy

Episode 8
"Confidence Man"

As time progresses on the Island, the medication the survivors have starts to run out. Shannon, who suffers from asthma, starts to have difficulties breathing due to the stress of not having an inhaler. It is rumored that Sawyer has extra inhalers, but is hoarding them away. When Jack confronts Sawyer, he is unwilling to give them up. Jack uses violence in an attempt to get the inhalers from him, and Sayid even tortures him, but all their attempts fail. Sawyer tells Jack that he will give up the

"I am the only Australian who loves peanut butter."

inhalers, but he will only give them to Kate. When Kate comes to get the inhalers, Sawyer changes his mind, and demands a kiss from her. Kate calls Sawyer out on trying too hard to be unlovable. Kate begins to realize that there is more to Sawyer than there appears to be. A letter that Sawyer carries around revels that Sawyer grew up with hardships. The letter exposes that Sawyers family was involved in a scandalous affair. Sawyer's mother had an affair with a man, who then asked her for money for an investment to get more money. His mother willingly gave the man the money, which he stole. Sawyer's father was outraged and killed his wife, and himself, leaving Sawyer an orphan.

A flashback reveals that Sawyer is in the exact same situation, only this time as the con man. After spending the night with a woman named Jessica,

"That was like – Jedi moment."

Sawyer reveals a briefcase full of money. Sawyer convinces Jessica and her husband to give him money for a deal that will triple their money in two weeks. As Sawyer goes to finalize the deal, Jessica's son walks into the room. Seeing the boy changes something in Sawyer, and he walks away from the deal. This moment changes Sawyer, because he realizes that he has become the man he hated. He has become the con man that breaks apart families. This thought shakes Sawyer from his con man ways and he abandons this life. Sawyer risked a lot by walking away from this deal, because he is indebted to someone who has threaten to kill him if he does not return the money he borrowed.

What is haunting you from your past?

_____

_____

_____

_____

Do you believe God can forgive you of your past sins?

_____

_____

_____

_____

Has someone else from your past done something to hurt you?

_____

_____

_____

_____

4. Will you forgive them?

_____

_____

_____

_____

"I became the man I was hunting."

It is necessary to decide what will define who you are. The best example of this is Saul of Tarsus. Known across the Middle East for his cruelty towards followers of Jesus and members of the arising church named The Way. Saul was appointed as Pharisee. The Jewish leaders gave him power to capture and torture the followers of Christ.

Saul has an encounter with God on the road to Damascus, and it shakes him from his way of life. Saul changes his name to Paul and begins preaching the Gospel to the Jews and the Gentiles. Paul changes his life mission, he is no longer persecuting Christians, but bringing the word of Jesus and encouraging those he was previously trying to kill. In a unique way, Paul became the man he used to hate. Joshua Loth Liebman said, "We achieve inner health only through forgiveness - the forgiveness not only of others but also of ourselves." Sometimes pressing forward is easier when we fix what was behind.

Another person who totally made a change was Zacchaeus. Luke 19 records this thief of a tax collector meeting Jesus and immediately having a changed heart. He promised to give half of his wealth to the poor and repay anyone he wronged four times over.

Likewise, Nicodemus went from hoarding wealth to a life of generosity. He didn't appreciate the graciousness of Jesus until the crucifixion. John 19:38-39 records, "Later, Joseph of Arimathea asked Pilate for the body of Jesus. Now Joseph was a disciple of Jesus, but secretly because he feared the Jewish leaders. With Pilate's permission, he came and took the body away. He was accompanied by Nicodemus, the man who earlier had visited Jesus at night. Nicodemus 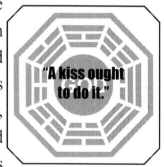 brought a mixture of myrrh and aloes, about seventy-five pounds." Nicodemus met with Jesus secretly, not willing to be known as a follower. Then he stepped out and changed. A Talmud of a rabbi records a story of Nicodemus' daughter begging in the street because he

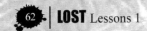

had given away all his wealth to charity. Sometimes it may be good to become the man we hated.

"We are products of our past, but we don't have to be prisoners of it"-
— Rick Warren

Chapter 9

■ ■ ■

180

Episode 9
"Solitary"

At the beginning of episode nine, Sayid is far away from camp walking on the beach when he comes across a wire. The wire intrigues him and he decides to follow it.

As Sayid continues to follow the wire into the jungle, he comes across a trip wire. He tries to step around it but a rope wraps around his ankle and lifts him upside down hanging from a nearby tree. He is hanging there all night until he hears someone in the darkness that cuts him down.

Sayid wakes up in a dark room underground bound down to a chair. He hears a woman repeatedly asking, "Where is Alex?" Sayid tries to explain why he was out in the jungle in that area, but the woman

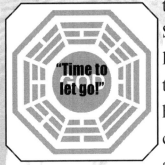

"Time to let go!"

techniques that he needs to let Shannon go and that he can still love her without always giving in to her every whim and rescuing her from every situation. Boone couldn't be free from his trials and heartache until he let go of the past and what happened with Shannon. We see the same thing happened to Abraham concerning his son Isaac in the Bible. Abraham would have to be willing to let go of his life's plans and one of the hardest things anyone could give up: his son.

Abraham was faithful to God and followed his commands and believed God's words and promises. God had promised to give the land of Canaan to Abraham and his decedents. God even blessed Abraham with a son in his old age, and Abraham loved his son dearly. God wanted to test that Abraham's love for Him was above all else. So one day he commanded Abraham to travel to Mount Moriah and offer his son up as a sacrifice. Abraham never doubted God and knew that there had to be a reason for this command. He trusted that God would not have him do that which was wrong, and even if he did kill his son, he believed God would raise him from the dead (Hebrews 11:17-19). So he only wants to know where Alex is. Sayid tries once more to explain that he is a survivor of a plane crash. As the conversation carries on, Sayid realizes that this is the French woman from the transmission that they picked

"Buy your ticket into Heaven?"

up. He finds out her name is Rousseau. The two talk for a while until Rousseau drugs Sayid in order to move him to a table to fix a music box that brought her peace when she first crashed on the island sixteen years ago.

At the beach, Jack finds out that Hurley has created a golf course on a grassy area of the island. At first Jack is angry that Hurley wasted his time doing this, but once Hurley explains the survivors need an activity that is fun to do in order to "let loose" he calms down. All the survivors migrate their way to the golf course and make bets with people about who will win. Sawyer even makes an appearance and attempts to socialize with the others after Kate recommends he make a better effort in doing so.

Once Sayid wakes up, he fixes the music box for Rousseau. Afterwards, Rousseau hears a noise coming from a trap nearby where they are staying. She leaves to investigate the disturbance and Sayid takes action. He escapes from his bounds and runs into the jungle with a rifle he steals from Rousseau's belongings. As he is running away, he sees Rousseau. Sayid aims his gun at her and begs her to let him go. She says she cannot because she does not want to be alone anymore. He fires his gun in fear of his life, but he realizes that the gun pin has been removed. Rousseau says she removed the pin after her old partner went crazy and tried to shoot her with it. Sayid begs her to let him go because he is not crazy. In the end, Rousseau lets him go back to the camp unharmed and without a struggle.

The story of Saul becoming Paul really relates with the transformation Sayid went through. In Acts 9, this transformation is described. Saul is first seen to have had intense hatred for all Christians. He persecuted and tortured any who claimed to be with Jesus. He was exactly the type of person that one may think that God would never use. Amazingly, one day,

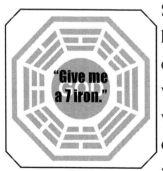
"Give me a 7 iron."

Saul experienced God. Saul and his acquaintances were walking down the road to Damascus, when suddenly; Saul was struck with a beam of light. He was directly addressed by the Lord, and told to change his ways.

After this collision with God, Saul drastically changed his lifestyle. One might say that he made a "180." That is, he stopped doing what he was doing, and completely changed how he lived his life for the better.

In LOST Sayid recognized that he had a problem with reverting to his past in regards to torturing people. The memories of his past had always haunted him. Sayid promised himself that he would try to never go back to the way he once was. Sadly, he broke this promise when

he used the bamboo chutes with Sawyer. Matthew 18:8 says, "If your hand or your foot causes you to stumble, cut it off and throw it away. It is better for you to enter life maimed or crippled than to have two hands or two feet and be thrown into eternal fire." Obviously Sayid did not go to such a drastic measure as to cut off his own hand or foot but he removed himself from people to relieve his temptation. In his excursion in the woods, he found himself. He made a full turn and decided to change his life.

Similarly, in our lives, we need to recognize if there is a serious problem, and fix it. George Elliot said, "No evil dooms us hopelessly except the evil we love, and desire to continue in, and make no effort to escape from." Many people are plagued with problems that hold them back as a person such as addiction and bad habits. As writer Oscar Wilde puts it, "I can avoid anything except temptation." Some of the strongest Christians are people who have gone through really tough phases in their lives. The key is to recognize that there is a problem, and get out of that situation. The problem is that we like our distractions and bad habits too much. Author Mark Twain says, "There is a charm about the forbidden that makes it unspeakably desirable." This ties in with our sin nature; we are all born sinners, we do bad things and we like them.

"Doctor playing golf ... cop eating a donut?"

We cannot escape these things by ourselves but only through salvation and being cleansed by Jesus's death on the cross can we be free. Eliminating distractions and issues in one's life can make for radical changes that can lead to a renewed relationship with God and an overall better state of life. The key to doing this is prayer. Matthew 26:41 states that we need to, "Watch and pray that you may not enter into temptation. The spirit indeed is willing, but the flesh is weak." We can avoid temptations and distractions but not through our doing. Ephesians 6:11 says, "Put on the full armor of God, so that you can take your stand against the devil's schemes." It can only be through God delivering us from the source of temptation or distraction.

Are there any relevant temptations in your life?

_____

_____

_____

_____

What and who are these temptations caused by?

_____

_____

_____

_____

How can you eliminate these temptations in your life?

_____

_____

_____

_____

How do you intend to carry out these steps?

_____

_____

_____

_____

When going gets tough, how will you stick to your guns?

_____

_____

_____

_____

"Everyone thinks about changing the world, but no one t hinks of changing himself."

– Leo Tolstoy

Chapter 10

■ ■ ■

It's the Choice that Counts

Episode 10
"Raised by Another"

The episode beings with Claire having a nightmare, she wakes up and hears a baby crying. She begins to panic and thinks something has happened and that someone attacked her. Claire's vision flashes back to when she first finds out she's pregnant. Claire and her boyfriend, Thomas, agree that having a baby and becoming a family "could be like, the best thing ever." As the episode continues, Thomas breaks up with Claire and she consults a psychic. The psychic convinces her to keep her baby, but if she adamantly does not want it, then she must take Flight 815 to Los

"We don't have to braid each other's hair."

Angeles. But as a pregnant woman sitting alone on an island after the flight crashed, she realized that this was not the best advice.

Sadly, Claire did not count the cost of her choices. The Bible talks many times about counting the cost. Luke 14:26-33 demonstrates how one person can be affected by the costs of a single decision. In the first half of the passage, the decision is to intentionally choose to commit all to Christ. Luke says that committing to the Lord means being able to let go of everything 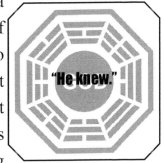 else in one's life. If the Lord asks something from His follower, he or she needs to be ready for whatever is required. This means that one should think through all the tasks that the Lord solicits. The Lord wants his children to be all in.

What is one difficult choice that you had to make for someone else or for yourself?

_____

_____

_____

_____

Name a time when your own choices have impacted another person, either in a positive or negative way:

_____

_____

_____

_____

The second part of the passage focuses more on the preparation involved with counting the cost. Verse 28 is a story about a person who decides to build a tower. Luke says, "'Suppose one of you wants to build a tower. Won't you first sit down and estimate the cost to see if you have enough money to complete it? For if

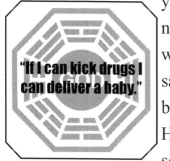

"If I can kick drugs I can deliver a baby."

you lay the foundation and are not able to finish it, everyone who sees it will ridicule you, saying, 'This person began to build and wasn't able to finish.'" Here, the passage speaks about someone starting a project

and then soon realizing that he does not have enough supplies to finish. To follow the Lord or complete a task for Him, one should think through whether or not he or she has the patience, time, and love to accept the difficult task.

Luke 9:23-26 is a short, yet very powerful passage. It simply states that one needs to be willing to let go of his or her passions and even one's life for the Lord. Everyone's purpose on the earth is to further the Kingdom of God. To be a follower of Christ one has to be willing to endure pain on earth. After giving themselves to the Lord, one will receive the greatest reward: being in community with the Lord forever.

As a believer, how has your choice to follow God impacted your life? If you are not a believer, if you chose this path, how would that choice affect your life?

_____

_____

_____

_____

If everyone made positive choices how would our world be different today?

_____

_____

_____

_____

A wise character from Harry Potter once said, "It is our choices, Harry, that show what we truly are, far more than our abilities." In this quote Dumbledore tells Harry that our choices are very important, even to the point of defining us. When, in Matthew 16:26, Matthew asks "What good will it be for someone to gain the whole world, yet forfeit their soul? Or what can anyone give in exchange for this soul?", he  is talking about a choice. This choice is keeping our soul safe and not exchanging it for anything else. The psychic tried to convince Claire to keep her baby and not give it up for adoption. This was a huge decision that she had to make.

A song by William J. Henry called "I'm Glad I Counted the Cost" says,

When first I started to seek the Lord,
I'm glad I counted the cost;
I fully measured to Jesus' Word;
I'm glad I counted the cost.

Here, Henry is singing about when he first started to seek the Lord, he counted the cost about what it meant.

He learned about the Word of God and "measured" what it would mean to become a follower. In the end, he says that he is glad that he counted the cost, and, near the end of the song, Henry says that he casts all his cares on God and is now blessed. Cast all your fears on the Lord and He will bear them for you.

Similarly, in a song by country singer Billy Dean, he sings,

It happens all around us
Each and every day
Someone's giving all they got
For someone else's sake
If you ever doubt it
Just think about the cross
When it comes to love,
you don't count the cost.

The moral of this song talks about how when people are in love, they do not count the cost. No matter who we are, we need to analyze and think through our plans. For the man who started to build a tower before counting the actual cost of his project, he was left in a stagnant place and in line of ridicule. Those who do not count the cost before their actions have to suffer the consequences no matter what. Claire says to the psychic, "If you're a psychic, why do you have to count it?" In reality, we all have to count the cost of every action we make, but if we believe in Jesus, He is there for us every step of the way.

"To give, and not to count the cost to fight, and not to heed the wounds, to toil, and not to seek for rest, to labor, and not to ask for any reward, save that of knowing that we do thy will"

– St. Ignatius of Loyola

Chapter 11

■ ■ ■

Two Trails

Episode 11
"All the Beşt Cowboys Have Daddy Issues"

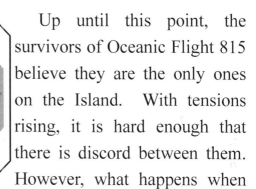

"He's leaving us a trail"

Up until this point, the survivors of Oceanic Flight 815 believe they are the only ones on the Island. With tensions rising, it is hard enough that there is discord between them. However, what happens when they realize that one of them was not on the plane. After reading the manifest, Hurley discovers that Ethan, an awkward introvert, was not on the list. Unfortunately, Ethan has already kidnapped Claire and Charlie before anyone figures out Ethan is an imposter. With Claire and Charlie taken, Jack along with Locke, Boone, and Kate, track down Ethan and rescue Charlie and Claire.

Before they leave in their rescue mission Jack has a flashback.

The familiar operating room, the beeping of the monitor, then silence: Jack has witnessed a terrible "mistake"- one that could have been prevented if the right choices were made. Jack sees someone who has chosen the wrong path, and succumbed to their shortcomings, filled with denial. He has two paths to follow, the right or the wrong. There are two paths in the woods, one that hopefully leads to Claire and Charlie, the other to nowhere. A poem by Robert Frost says, "Two roads diverged in a wood and I took the one less traveled by, and that has made all the difference." Will Jack choose the road that is less traveled by? It is a matter of decision now.

In Jeremiah 42, the people of Judah find themselves in a predicament. Their lands have been oppressed by the unstoppable Babylonian nation for some time, but they are now ready to turn a new leaf. They must  make a decision on whether or not to stay in the land of Judah or move to the prosperous and safe land of Egypt. The people seek Jeremiah to gain advice from God, and after ten days of waiting, Jeremiah returns with an answer. God gave the people two options. They could stay in the land of Judah with His promise of protection, or the people could go to Egypt where they would surely perish.

The situation in the book of Jeremiah parallels what is happening to Jack in this LOST episode. The people had a decision to make. One could save lives and ensure safety; the other was full of uncertainty and danger. Sometimes we find ourselves in the same situation, struggling to make the right decision or "follow the correct path." God gives us a choice, but we must be willing to follow His plan. For example, we have two paths we could follow. One is the path of God that may seem dangerous at times, and the other path is one without God that can give a sense of safety. However, through faith, we are safer following the path of God because of His protection over us. Therefore, His way is the best way. God's way is the way that blesses and brings joy to those who abide by it.

Two choices are given to us in life. The first choice is to follow our own desires, which could lead us anywhere. Secondly, we are given the choice to follow God's plan that will lead us

"Sorry, fresh out of sweet forgiveness"

down a path of righteousness. Proverbs 12:28 says, "In the way of righteousness there is life; along that path is immortality." Many people choose the path that appears to be the easiest. The right choice may be harder,

"Looks like you fixed everything but the patient"

but in the long run, turn out to be better. Matthew 7:13-14 says, "Enter through the narrow gate. For wide is the gate and broad is the road that leads to destruction, and many enter through it. But small is the gate and narrow the road that leads to life, and only a few find it." The people who choose the path of righteousness will be rewarded because they chose the path to follow God.

Psalms 119:105 says, "Your word is a lamp for my feet, a light on my path." As humans we aren't perfect. God understands that! He provides us with the Holy Spirit to guide us. We know we are on the right path when our conscience is actively working in our hearts. With God's word, we will be able to make the right decision that is pleasing to God.

Jack and Kate chose the right path to find Charlie. However, they were too late, because Charlie was hanging from the tree with a noose around his neck.

Charlie was presumed dead, but Jack did not accept the fate of Charlie. Hurrying to the hanging, lifeless man, Jack and Kate cut the rope and prepare to resuscitate him. Jack was not going to give up like his father did in his flashback. His father chose the wrong path by drinking alcohol before a major surgery that resulted in the death of the patient. After the death of the patient, Jack's father lies to cover up his mistake. Jack tried to save the patient his father irreparably harmed by going into the operating room under the influence. It was too late; Jack could not save the patient. Because of his father's wrongdoings, the patient died. Ethan's wrongdoings nearly killed Charlie, but like before with Jack's father's patient, he attempted to resuscitate Charlie, but this time he was successful in bringing him back.

Many times we are given multiple paths; however, there is only one "right" path. Several connections are made between the Bible and LOST that deal with choosing the right path. In conclusion, we find that almost everyone will have a choice. No matter how difficult the path is, when you choose God's path, you will have chosen the right path. When the wrong path is chosen, consequences will follow.

What signs or signals tell us that we are on the right path? How do we know we are on the right path?

_____

_____

_____

_____

If you are following the wrong path, does God allow you to switch paths to the path of righteousness?

_____

_____

_____

_____

3. Does God follow us even when we are on the wrong path, or are we alone?

_____

_____

_____

_____

"Older and wiser voices can help you find the right path, if only you are willing to listen."
– Jimmy Buffett

Chapter 12

■ ■ ■

Inside Out

Episode 12
"Whatever the Case May Be"

Episode 12, "Whatever the Case May Be", finds Sawyer and Kate discovering a beautiful, glistening waterfall and pool. After messing around for a bit, they discover that this beautiful pool is not so beautiful on the inside; Sawyer and Kate soon discover the lake has a couple of corpses rotting in it. In this macabre pool, Kate discovers her missing silver case, but is unable to open it because the key is missing. The episode then moves to Kate's flashbacks of the bank robbery. Kate appears as an innocent loan customer, but turns out to be in cahoots with the thieves the whole time, all for the contents

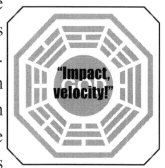

of a mystery safety deposit box. Back on the Island, the whole issue of what is in the case develops throughout the rest of the episode. Kate and Jack dig up the case key from the marshall's body; Kate tells Jack what is in the case, but is obviously leaving something out. The whole episode is spent wondering what is in the case. What is in the case? A dark reminder of the man Kate loved and killed. Episode 12 of LOST is filled with the big mystery of what is really on the inside, and does it match up to its outward appearance.

"Woe to you, teachers of the law and Pharisees, you hypocrites! You are like whitewashed tombs, which look beautiful on the outside but on the inside are full of the bones of the dead and everything unclean." (Matthew 23:27). Listen to this! Whitewashed tombs are beautiful on the outside, but full of dead bones on the inside. This verse shows the exact truth of our world. We live in a generation where all we want is to be beautiful, just like all of the celebrities. Guess who

"The easiest way isn't always the best"

sets the standards? The people on TV, the models on the hottest magazines, and, of course, the musicians producing the rhythms of our society. They set the so-called laws of fashion, beauty, and personality. They are the trendsetters, the "cool" people. Those people are all so caught up in their outer selves, rather than who they are on the inside.

Let's just take a step back to look and see who we are, and what we have become. Sometimes it may not be all that pretty - maybe you feel empty. Maybe your whole life you have struggled with insecurities or identity problems, or you have humility issues. Proverbs 31:30 says, "Charm is deceptive, and beauty is fleeting; but a woman who fears the Lord is to be praised." Here it says charm, nor beauty matter: just fear God. Matthew 6:25 says, "Therefore I tell you, do not worry about your life, what you will eat or drink; or about your body, what you will wear. Is not life more than food, and the body more than clothes?" None of these outer appearances matter; all that matters is what is on the inside.

So many people strive to be something they are not and never end up getting anywhere. It is plain and simple, 1 Peter 5:6-7 says, "So be content with who you are, and don't put on airs. God's strong hand is on you; he'll promote you at the right time. Live carefree before God; he is most careful with you." It's so simple - God has laid it all out. All you have to do is be yourself and follow along the path God has made for you. It will be hard work, and trials and temptations will stand in your way, but God has a bigger plan for you. Just like how Adam and Eve were in the Garden and everything was perfect. They were given strict orders not to eat the fruit from the Tree of the Knowledge of Good and Evil, but they were tempted and ate the fruit. They were no longer perfect, and they were cast away.. Do not let yourself be like the fruit from that tree - you will never be completely filled with only outer beauty. There will always be emptiness without God.

The temptation or tendency is to cover up our ugly side. Helen Cross said, "Her words were like tin foil; they shone and they covered things up." God calls us to be transparent and real. We need to clean up, not cover up.

God calls each and every one of us to a life of selfless humility. Luke 14:10-11 (MSG) says, "When you're invited to dinner, go and sit at the last place. Then when the host comes he may very well say, 'Friend, come up to the front.' That will give the dinner something to talk about! What I am saying is, if you walk around with your nose in the air, you're going to end up flat on your face. But if you are content to be simply yourself, you will become more than yourself." This verse shows humility; do not think of yourself better than anyone else. We were all created equal, and no one is better than another. People sometimes tend to look at the "outcasts" and think of themselves better than them. They only look at the outer

"Heavenly Father, we thank you"

appearance, because they never took the chance to get to know them. These so-called "outcasts" may have more of a heart towards people than most, but because they are shutdown all the time through the oppression of the selfish, they never have a chance to prove themselves. Often people like this give up because of those who are only interested in themselves. Their spirit is inevitably crushed, and the love they show is oppressed as well. Suntzu went so far as to say, "Appear weak when you are strong and strong when you are weak."

We need to look deeper into people rather than how they look or how they act. This world does not give anyone a chance if they do not live up to the celebrity's standards or have their outward appearance. This issue is growing day-by-day and becomes more and more prevalent as our world becomes stuck in the deathtrap of sin. People are so caught up in society and the desire to be like somebody else that they miss what God has for them. Everything is backwards in this world. It is time to bring the inside out so people can get to know the real us: the humble, the loving, the compassionate, and the godly us that was fearfully and wonderfully made in His own image.

Take a second to examine yourself. Are you more focused on the inside or outside?

_____

_____

_____

_____

How can you focus on what God has for you instead of being caught up in this world?

_____

_____

_____

_____

Why are you so quick to judge a person before you even know him?

_____

_____

_____

_____

How can you work on seeing people for who they really are?

_____

_____

_____

_____

What are some ways you can humble yourself?

_____

_____

_____

_____

"The opposite of talking isn't listening. The opposite
of talking is waiting."

– Fran Lebowitz

Chapter 13

■ ■ ■

Let Go, Let God!

Episode 13
"Hearts and Minds"

"Hearts and Minds" is a challenging episode that focuses on the torturous pain that is involved in letting go of something that one has clung on to for too long. The struggle between what Boone knows and what Boone feels is made evident through the way that he is continuously rescuing his manipulative and deceitful stepsister because of his love for her. Boone experiences a metamorphosis of sorts throughout the episode: he starts off as a jealous father-figure who warns Sayid to stay away from his sister and ends up as a more mature man who realizes that for once his sister has made a decent choice, and he can continue to love her in a healthier and more natural way. Boone learns with the help of Locke's somewhat questionable

rose early that morning and gathered firewood and got Isaac and headed towards Mount Moriah on his donkey. As he arrived at the mountain, he built the alter. As Isaac watched him, he said "My father" and Abraham replied, "Here I am my son." Isaac responded, "Behold the fire and the wood: but where is the lamb for the burnt offering?" Abraham answered, "My son God will provide Himself a lamb for a burnt offering" (Genesis 22 KJV). When the altar was done being built, Isaac was tied up and placed upon it. As Abraham went to cast a blow upon his son, which would end his son's life, God spoke, "Lay not thine hand upon the lad, neither do thou a thing unto him; for now I know that thou fearest God, seeing that thou hast not withheld thy son, thine some only from Me." Abraham lowered his hand and turned to see a ram caught in the thicket. He used the lamb in place of his son as a sacrifice to God.

It probably wasn't easy for Abraham to be willing to sacrifice his son. There must have been a serious war going on in his head: whether to obey God and give Him control or to do what he wanted for his future and have a son and many nations of generations. But Abraham

"Be careful what you wish for"

made the right choice: he gave control to God and was blessed because of it. Just as Abraham had to let go and give control to God, we too have to do the same thing in our lives. Abraham had to let go of his plans in life: to have a son, to have grandchildren, to have many nations. As soon as he did, he was blessed; he was able to keep his son, and he was blessed having many nations.

Abraham's story is not the only place in the Bible that tells us we need to let go. Proverbs 3:5-6 says, "Trust in the Lord with all your heart and lean not on your own understanding; in all your ways submit to him, and he will make your paths straight." God's way won't always  be the easiest way; sometimes it will be the hardest way; but sometimes the hardest way is the best way you can communicate with God. C.S. Lewis once said, "We can ignore even pleasure. But pain insists upon being attended to. God whispers to us in our pleasures, speaks in our conscience, but shouts in our pains: it is his megaphone to rouse a deaf world." This pretty much talks about how in happy times we can seem to forget about it quite easily; but pain is something hard for us to ever forget about. In the good, we might not be listening for God or "paying attention" to Him; but it is in our time of pain, when we call out to Him that we hear His voice the loudest.

What trials are you facing in your life?

____

____

____

____

What are some of the things that you can't afford to not have control of?

____

____

____

____

When we let go of what we "can't live without" and our past sufferings, it's amazing what God can do and what He reveals to us! Jeremiah 29:11-13 says, "For I know the plans I have for you," declares the Lord, "plans to prosper you and not to harm you, plans to give you hope and a future. Then you will call on me and come and pray to me, and I will listen to you.

You will seek me and find me when you seek me with all your heart." He knows what your purpose is in this life, and He will bless you and direct you in ways you would have never imagined. You just have to take the first step: Let Him in, and give Him control.

How can you start letting God take control in your life?

_____

_____

_____

_____

It's hard sometimes to let God have control; we may be fearful or uncertain, and even doubt God; but when God has control, He can handle any situation, nothing is impossible with God! Philippians 4:6-7 says, "Do not be anxious about anything, but in every situation, by prayer and petition, with thanksgiving, present your requests to God. And the peace of God, which transcends all understanding, will guard your hearts and your minds in Christ Jesus." When we let go and give God the control of every aspect of our lives, we become new. We can start living for Him and the plan He has for us. We can leave the hardships and suffering of the past in the past, we can have a chance to start a whole new life. Like Gandhi once said, "You may never know what results come of your action, but if you do nothing there will be no result." It all starts with one simple step: Let Him in. Give God control.

In what ways will God take control in your life? In what ways will you be able to start new?

_____

_____

_____

_____

Your charm has inspired an secret admirer.

: "The more we let God take us over, the more truly ourselves we become - because He made us. He invented us. He invented all the different people that you and I were intended to be...It is when I turn to Christ, when I give up myself to His personality, that I first begin to have a real personality of my own."

– CS Lewis

Chapter 14

■ ■ ■

#Shepherd

Episode 14
"Special"

In this episode of LOST, the focus is directed at the background story of Michael and his son Walt. While Michael is having flashbacks and constantly getting upset by Walt spending a significant

"You guys up for some golf?"

amount of time on the island with Locke, Charlie is struggling with his curiosity about Claire's diary. Charlie has recently had some strong feelings for Claire especially since she has been kidnapped by Ethan. He then decides he will carefully monitor and protect Claire's diary, along with her other belongings, until she returns. Although his intention is to protect her personal feelings and thoughts from others on the Island, he is curious himself to what Claire could have possibly written about him. This curiosity eventually tempts Charlie to read what Claire had written in her diary. He is happy with what he reads.

The idea of protection is a major topic of the Bible. God showed protection to his chosen people, the Israelites, in times of trouble with war (1 Samuel 17), and protected his own son from King Herod (Matthew 2:13-18), the ruler of Rome. He protected all of the Israelites when they were escaping from Egypt (Exodus 14), and he also would protect just one servant, Noah (Genesis 7:6-10), from a devastating flood. It is made obvious that God values protection and did not hesitate to send his angels down to earth to help with our protection. Yet, how important is it to God to protect other people's possessions? Well, in 1 Samuel 25, David and his army are going after a man who insulted David's name. In verse 13 it says, "… about four hundred men went up with David, while two hundred stayed with the supplies." It seems obvious to leave men behind during battle so as not to be attacked yourself, but God gives a little more insight on this, 5 chapters later. In chapter 30, David and his army reach the city of Ziklag where they find it destroyed from the Amalekites and all the wives and children taken captive. David's army is on the brink of disaster as some of them have pondered stoning him as they were bitter about the loss of their families. However, David chose to pursue the Amalekites in hope of rescuing the captives. When David expressed his plan, again two hundred men stayed behind to protect the camp, but this time it says that, "two hundred of them were too exhausted to cross the valley, but David and the other four hundred continued the pursuit" (1 Samuel 10). First

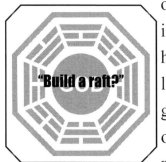
"Build a raft?"

of all, these men must have been in some bad shape if they did not have the energy to pursue their loved ones, and the men that did go must have been pretty worn out themselves. However, these men obviously had the help of God as they caught up with the raiding party that night and fought all the time until the next night. They killed all of the Amalekites except for four hundred who fled from battle, and they recovered everything that had been taken as well as what they had taken from their other raids. As David and the army returned and came to the two hundred who had stayed behind, some of David's men said that they should only be allowed to take back their family, but none of the plunder. However, David's reply to this was, "The share of the man who stayed with the supplies is to be the same as that of him who went down to the battle. All will share alike. David made this a statute and ordinance for Israel from that day to this" (1 Samuel 30:24-25). God makes it clear to us through his servant David that it is important to protect the possessions of others while they are gone and should be valued no less than the task of the person they are watching it for.

So what does all of this have to do with the average person who is not stranded on an island? Protection of God's possessions is what this is all about. In this

"Taking control of our destiny"

episode of LOST, Charlie has feelings for Claire and while she is gone, he decides to protect her possessions from everyone else on the Island. The men who stay behind love their fellow soldiers and their families. Staying back to protect their possessions is a very important task. The theme that seems to be apparent is that if you love someone, you want to keep what is theirs safe from harm until they return. God created the universe, Earth and everything in it. He sent his own son to die on the cross for our sins because he loves us more than we can comprehend. God expects us to take care of what He has left behind for us. What exactly did God leave behind for us? He left behind His greatest creations! What are His greatest creations? The human race! Genesis 1:27 says, "So God created mankind in his own image, in the image of God he created them; male and female he created them." God expects us to take care and protect one another until He returns. Matthew 24:30 says, "At that time the sign of the Son of Man will appear in the sky, and all the nations of the earth will mourn. They will see the Son of Man coming on the clouds of the sky, with power and great glory." Jesus is definitely returning for what he left behind!

Now what does protecting each other really mean? Protecting one another could be taken in many different ways. For example, a loving husband would protect his family at any cost. This could mean financially, emotionally or physically. That husband would never want to see anything bad happen to the family he loves so much. There is also a very different way to view our job of protecting others until God returns. We must spread the word of God, and let all who have not heard of Jesus Christ a chance to learn of what he did for us on the cross. By doing this, we are protecting everyone who has not heard of Jesus from the terrible fate that awaits them if they do not accept God by the time He returns. If someone forgot their wallet, they would hope that everything that was inside would still be there when they returned for it. God wants all of His creation to love Him, and He wants all of us to return to Him when Jesus returns. Charles Stanley said, "Too many Christians have a commitment of convenience. They'll stay faithful as long as it's safe and doesn't involve risk, rejection, or criticism. Instead of standing alone in the face of challenge or temptation, they check to see which way their friends are going." The task that God has left behind for us is a very difficult one, but it is something that must be done. We must protect each other until God returns.

Can you think of a time in your life when you needed to protect something sacred?

_____

_____

_____

_____

What is something that did not belong to you, but you knew that it was your responsibility to protect it? What would you sacrifice to protect that object?

_____

_____

_____

_____

How could you use that same strategy to protect the Bible and your faith?

_____

_____

_____

_____

Who could you protect by sharing the gospel of Jesus Christ?

_____

_____

_____

_____

"I cannot think of any need in childhood as strong as the need for a father's protection."

– Sigmund Freud

Chapter 15

■ ■ ■

Castaway

Episode 15
"Homecoming"

Episode 15 starts off with the long-awaited return of Claire to the campsite. Although everyone is relieved that Claire and her baby are okay, it soon becomes evident that she has lost all memory of the plane crash, and all of the people she came to know on the Island. Charlie is most shocked by Claire's memory loss and is saddened when he realizes she doesn't remember their friendship. In the attempt to boost Claire's memory, Charlie hands Claire her diary, and she asks, "Are we friends?" Charlie then explains to Claire that Ethan took them both. After Claire returns to the site, Ethan reappears to Charlie and threatens him. This sets the whole camp into turmoil, and they later devise a plan to capture Ethan. During the manhunt for Ethan, all four men find him and have four guns pointed at him ready to interrogate, but suddenly, Ethan is shot 6 times and falls dead to the ground, killed by Charlie. Later that night after everything died down, Claire approaches Charlie and says, "I remember peanut butter" and explains that she wants to trust him.

As the survivors are under attack, Jack suggests that the survivors should all group up in the cave and set up defenses. Then Locke says, "What if he wants us to gather together so he can slaughter us like sheep." Often referred to as the sheep of the Great Shepherd, Christians have been and still are under constant attack from other people and things. Jesus Christ and eleven of his twelve apostles were martyred for spreading Christianity. In the modern world, Christians  are still under attack by other religions, temptations, hardship, and more. As it is written "For your sake, we face death all day long; we are considered as sheep to be slaughtered" (Roman 8:36). However, we should not be drawn away from God because of the trouble, the hardship or the persecution. We should be united and conquer the challenges through the love of Jesus

Christ.

Claire, in this episode, becomes an outsider in the community. One cannot help but notice the resemblance of Claire to the Woman at the Well in John 4. Ethan, one of the others, threatens to kill one survivor each day till the survivors give Claire to him. When Claire goes to the fountain to get water, she is treated differently. She notices people are staring at her in a hostile way, and people are avoiding starting a conversation with her. Claire is an outcast of her community. In the Bible story, the Samaritan woman is getting water from the well. She too is an outcast from her community. She is shunned and rejected by the other woman for her immorality.

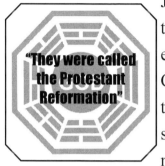

"They were called the Protestant Reformation"

Just like the Women at the Well and Claire, Christians are often cast out because of what we believe. Once we are reborn as Christians, we are labeled as someone else, someone who changes his or her ways for God. Once we are renewed as a Christian, our lives are not going to be as fine and dandy as he imagined. Christians go through the same things that normal people do, but we can also be cast out or rejected. Jesus was also rejected, as it states in John 1:10-11, "He was in the world, and though the world was made through him, the world did not recognize him. He came to that which was his own, but his own did not receive him." Do not be worried about being an outcast, because all Christians are outcasts; we are all looked at as different and rejected. As Christians, we cannot stay in this position of being an outcast or being rejected by others. Daniel Radcliffe has said, "There is something inherently valuable about being a misfit."

The Bible tells us to go out to the world and speak the truth to the lost in Mark 16:15, saying, "He said to them, "Go into all the world and preach the gospel to all creation." Some people are going to accept what you have to say or just reject what you have to say because of their past or certain beliefs they ready have; just as Jesus got rejected we are going to be rejected too. As Christians, we are called to be the light to the world. Matthew 5:14-15 says, "You are the light of the world. A town built on a hill cannot be hidden. Neither do people light a lamp and put it under a bowl. Instead they put it on its stand, and it gives light to everyone in the house." God calls us to be this light, but we can't do this if we stay in the state of being an outcast - we have to be the light. There are many people in the world

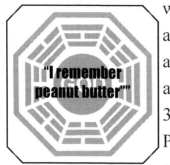

"I remember peanut butter'"

with different personalities, we as Christians need to be bold and preach the gospel to this lost and broken world. Acts 28:30-31 says, "For two whole years Paul stayed there in his own rented house and welcomed all who came to see him. He proclaimed the kingdom of God and taught about the Lord Jesus Christ—with all boldness and without hindrance!" often we are rejected in our society, but we should not feel that we have lost because Psalm 94:14 says, "For the Lord will not reject his people; he will never forsake his inheritance." Those who reject us, also reject God. God does not reject His people. Joseph Conrad said, "Who knows what true loneliness is-not the conventional word but the naked terror? To the lonely themselves it wears a mask. The most miserable outcast hugs some memory or some illusion." Having God at our side is not an illusion. We can walk, but never alone.

Do you ever have a fear of being rejected? If you do, how do you cope with it?

_____

_____

_____

_____

How do you deal with rejection?

_____

_____

_____

_____

What motivates you to keep trying to spread God's words?

_____

_____

_____

_____

"Some of us aren't meant to belong. Some of us have to turn the world upside down and shake it until we make our own place in it."

–Elizabeth Lowell

Chapter 16

■ ■ ■

Burned

Episode 16
"Outlaws"

Episode 16 begins with Sawyer finding that his possessions have been destroyed by a wild boar. Sawyer angrily chases the boar into the jungle, but it escapes without a trace. Sawyer decides to go back into the jungle to hunt the wild boar with the help of Kate. In the jungle, they encounter Locke, who tells them a strange story which reminds Sawyer of the reason why he came to Sydney. When Sawyer was a boy, his parents had both died tragically because of one con man's fraud. Ironically, Sawyer had become a con man, he had grown into the man he hates most. A flashback

"Will it ease your suffering?"

shows Sawyer being informed that the con man who caused his parent's death is living in Sydney and Sawyer goes there to avenge himself. Meanwhile, on the beach, Charlie is shaken by Ethan's death, leaving him a quiet and disturbed man. The other characters are worried about his condition and try to find him help.

In Sydney, Sawyer finds himself at a bar with Dr. Christian Shephard, Jack's dad. Dr. Shephard has lost everything, including his relationship with his son, because of his drinking habits. He flees to Sydney, telling Sawyer that it is "the closest you can get to hell without being burned." At the bar, he has a chance to go to the payphone and fix his relationship with his son, but he is too weak to make the call. After Sawyer talks to Dr. Shephard, he goes out and kills the con man in order to ease his own suffering, only to find out that it was the wrong man. In the present, Sawyer finally finds the boar near a quagmire but for some reason he lowers the gun and lets the boar live. On the beach, Charlie receives help from Sayid, who says to Charlie, "You're not alone. Don't pretend to be."

"I never..wore pink"

This episode makes many strong connections to the

story of Lot in Genesis. In Genesis 13, Abram (not yet Abraham) and his nephew Lot are traveling south together as they leave Egypt. Both Lot and Abram are very rich in cattle, flocks, silver, and gold, but the land is unable to support both of them together. Both Lot and Abram have many servants and their servants have begun to fight and quarrel with each other. To avoid conflict between their servants, Lot and Abram decide to separate. Abram says to Lot, "Let's not have any quarreling between you and me, or between your herders and mine, for we are close relatives. Is not the whole land before you? Let's part company. If you go to the left, I'll go to the right; if you go to the right, I'll go to the left." (Genesis 13:8-9). Lot looks out over the land and sees that the plain of Jordan is a good, watered land and chooses that for himself. He leaves Abram and makes his new home near the city of Sodom.

Unfortunately, Sodom is a very wicked city filled with many wicked people who have sinned greatly against God. God was going to destroy Sodom because of its wickedness, but Abraham pleads with God on Lot's behalf. God sends angels to warn Lot to take his wife and two daughters out of the city before he destroys it. As they are leaving, the angels warn them not to look back; however, Lot's wife turns for one last look and instantly becomes a pillar of salt. Lot takes his daughters with him to live in a cave in the mountains. In this cave, the daughters perform shameful acts, which have great consequences on their descendants. Lot chooses to live in an evil city with bad people, and even though he is good, his family still suffers as a result of the corruption of Sodom. The entire story can be found in Genesis 13, 18 and 19.

The story of Lot and the episode "Outlaws" have much in common. In the episode, Sawyer makes a conscious decision to immerse himself in the world of crime and conning. This leads him to become more and more involved in this world of corruption. Likewise, Lot intentionally places himself near Sodom, and though he mostly resists, his entire family becomes tainted by the wickedness of the city. As stated by game developer Ken Levine, "We all make choices, but in the end our choices make us." The choices made by Sawyer and Lot both become fundamental to who they are. Sawyer's involvement with the criminal scene leads him to become desensitized to the evil happening, and he readily partakes in sinful acts to do his job, even going as far as to kill a man. Lot's family also falls into a similar situation, as sin becomes less of an issue in their eyes.

As the people in both the episode and in the Bible spend more time immersed in sin, they find it more difficult to escape. Sawyer requires a plane crash to get out of the business; Lot needs three angels to come and  remove him from Sodom. One wrong decision and sin can quickly escalate into inescapable mire. As entrepreneur Thomas Peterffy said, "You bend the rules a little bit and then it's a slippery slope." If sin and temptation take control, it can be nearly impossible to leave one's sin behind. However, it is essential to leave a life of sin, or else you will be burned. Sawyer finds himself in a world of regret that he cannot escape no matter how hard he tries. Lot's wife is turned into a pillar of salt, and his daughters found a line of people at war with the Israelites for years. This sinful "playing with fire" is addressed in Proverbs 6:27-28: "Can a man scoop fire into his lap without his clothes being burned? Can a man walk on hot coals without his feet being scorched?" The truth is that it is impossible to be in a life of sin without being burned in the end. This burning leaves scars that are not easy to remove.

Fortunately, as Sayid says to Charlie, "You're

"That's why the Sox will never win the Series"

not alone." Talking with others about the sins you struggle with is a great way to ease your way out of this slippery slope. Of course, the best way to avoid sin is to listen to the words of Psalms 1:1-2: "Blessed is the one who does not walk in step with the wicked or stand in the way that sinners take or sit in the company of mockers, but whose delight is in the law of the Lord, and who meditates on his law day and night." In the end, the answer is simple. How do you avoid sin? "Submit yourselves, then, to God. Resist the devil, and he will flee from you" (James 4:7). By devoting your life to God, you can avoid the pain and misery that are a result of playing with fire. The goal is not to get as close to hell as you can without being burned; it is to stay as far away from hell as possible. This can only be done by being with God in His Word and avoiding environments of sin. Is this easier said than done? Yes, but the result is very rewarding.

Do you find yourself stuck in sin like Sawyer or Lot's family was?

_____

_____

_____

_____

Do you have any permanent scars that are a result of a life of sin?

_____

_____

_____

_____

What can you do to let God bring you out of that situation and heal you?

_____

_____

_____

_____

How do you think God feels about people using His name to draw attention away from Him and to themselves?

_____

_____

_____

_____

What can we, as Christians, do to spread the light of the Lord?

_____

_____

_____

_____

"Sometimes you don't know you've crossed a line until you're already on the other side."

—Anonymous

Chapter 17

■ ■ ■

What Goes Around...

Episode 17
"...In Translation"

In episode seventeen of LOST, the viewer is exposed to the true backstory of Jin. The episode begins with Jin talking to Sun's father. Jin wants to ask for Sun's hand in marriage and tells Sun's father that

"She is my dream"

he is willing to do anything for her hand in marriage. Before giving his answer, Sun's father asks about how Jin's father feels about the marriage; Jin replies that he is dead. Sun's father is hesitant at first, but when he sees how much Jin cares about Sun, he accepts. After the flashback, the audience is back on the Island and sees Sun wearing a bikini. Jin rushes over to cover Sun and scorns her. Michael tries to defend Sun, but Sun slaps Michael. Michael leaves to continue work on the raft which, that same night was found engulfed in flames. Michael blames Jin for burning the raft, so Sawyer and Michael go to look for Jin. Sawyer finds Jin and beats him badly. Sawyer brings Jin to Michael so that they can decide. Just before Michael throws his fist at Jin, Sun steps in to defend Jin using her English. Everyone including Jin is surprised at Sun's secret. After the group leaves Sun and Jin, Sun asks for Jin's forgiveness, but he refuses. The final back story of Jin surfaces showing Jin returning to his proposed dead father asking for his forgiveness. Jin's father forgives him like nothing ever happened. Jin's father finishes by telling Jin to run away to Los Angles with Sun to save his marriage.

Have you ever thought that you have done something that could not be forgiven? Jin goes through the same predicament in this episode of LOST. In Jin's struggle to win Sun's father's approval, Jin disowns his own father. In Jin and Sun's society, lower class people could not marry those in the upper class, so Jin had to lie. Jin was so ashamed of his lie that he felt he could not return to his father.

"Everyone gets a new life on this island"

However, he was desperate for advice from his father, and, in return, he also received unintended forgiveness. Jin's situation is similar to that of the parable Jesus told about the Prodigal son. In Luke 15:11-32, a son takes his inheritance and uses it all on greed, lust, and gluttony. Eventually, the son runs out of money and sees that he needs to come back home to his father. The son hopes that his father will at least allow him to be a servant in his household. When the son first appears, walking towards his father's estate, the father runs to meet his son. The father tells his servants to prepare a feast for the arrival of his son, and all of the son's transgressions are washed away. Jin got caught up in work, and was lead off the right path. Desperate, he returned to his father, who forgave him for all that he had done. With his father's forgiveness, Jin set out to do the right thing. The Bible also provides more examples of forgiveness. One example would be Matthew 18:21-22 21, "Then Peter came to Jesus and asked, "Lord, how many times shall I forgive my brother or sister who sins against me? Up to seven times?", Jesus answered, "I tell you, not seven times, but seventy-seven times." This verse shows us that we need to forgive without ceasing, even when people do terrible things. C.S. Lewis stated once, "To be a Christian means to forgive the inexcusable because God has forgiven the inexcusable in you." God is the ultimate forgiver.

Jin got caught in his job and ended up doing some very bad things. Doing these things started to affect Jin's outlook on life. He realized he needed to rethink why he was doing this job, and evaluate the consequences the job has produced. He came to the

realization that no good was going to come from this job and that he needed to get away. Alison Croggon said, "We are all mistaken sometimes; sometimes we do wrong things, things that have bad consequences. But it does not mean we are evil, or that we cannot be trusted ever afterward." The quote by Croggon can also apply to Jin while they are on the Island in regards to Sun. Sun held the fact that she could speak English and did not let him know how close she was getting with the other people on the Island. While what she did was not right at all, Jin needs to realize that she can still be trusted, and deserves his forgiveness.

Matthew 18:21-35 illustrates a story about an owner and a servant. The servant owed the owner some money for which he did not have the money to repay him. The servant begged at the owner's feet so the owner was merciful and forgave the servant's debt. Later on, a very similar situation occurred with the servant. One of the servant's workers owed him money. The worker had no way to pay him back, but this time the servant was unmerciful and threw him into jail. The servant was forgiven, but he still was not able to forgive. The servant's actions did backfire, and he was punished. This illustrates how we need to always be willing to forgive others because we ourselves have been forgiven. Jin begs for forgiveness from his father, and his father grants it to him. In a turn of events, when Sun is begging for forgiveness from Jin, he refuses to forgive her. You cannot accept forgiveness from someone, if you refuse to give it to someone else.

Is there someone whom you need to forgive right now?

_____

_____

_____

_____

If you were in place of Jin's father, would you forgive him?

_____

_____

_____

_____

Can you forgive right away or does it take you time to forgive?

_____

_____

_____

_____

Has forgiving someone helped rebuild a relationship?

_____

_____

_____

_____

What are some things that hold you back from forgiving?

_____

_____

_____

_____

How does it make you feel to know that while God forgives you for your sin, you are refusing to forgive someone right now?

_____

_____

_____

_____

"The weak can never forgive. Forgiveness is the attribute of the strong."-
–Mahatma Gandhi

Chapter 18

■ ■ ■

Making Your Own Luck

Episode 18
"Numbers"

Episode 18, "Numbers," starts out with a flashback to Hurley winning the lottery. Everything seems to be going his way, until strange things begin to happen whenever he is around. People dying, houses burning, and false arrests are just a few of the events that take place. Hurley develops a theory that this set of numbers (4, 8, 15, 16, 23, 42) must be cursed. Hurley traces the numbers back to an acquaintance's friend and ends up talking to his wife, since the friend, Sam, killed himself

"I'm a big guy, I get dehydrated easy"

a few years back. She says that Hurley is looking for an excuse that doesn't exist. On the Island, Hurley rummages through some of Rousseau's stolen maps Sayid has. He finds the "cursed" numbers written on them. Hurley goes on a quest to find Rousseau in hopes she can explain that the same numbers are found on her maps. In the meantime, Sun and Jin have relationship problems and are struggling to work things out. When Hurley finally reaches Rousseau, she explains that the numbers are what brought her to the Island. Hurley is relieved and he has a new sense of closure because he is not crazy. The closing scene of the episode pans to the same numbers that are engraved on the hatch. Are the numbers really cursed?! What do they mean?!

Some people in life believe they are cursed, while others believe they make their own luck. The Bible addresses this in Matthew 25: 13- 30 in the parable of the three servants. One servant was given five bags of silver, and he invested and made it into ten. The next was given 2 bags of silver, and he made it into four bags. The last servant was given one bag, and he did not invest, but instead he buried it in the ground and came back with no more money than he was given before. I think it is safe to say that no one wants to be

"4, 8, 15, 16, 23, 42"

remembered as the person who did nothing with what God gave him. Not every person will have the same potential and abilities. As we were told in the parable, some will be given more than others. So, though some will have more talents than others, it is what we do with God's gifts that's important.

Many people pray for things to happen, but then they do not do anything to make it happen. They want to sit back and use the excuse, "I'm waiting for God to help me," or," I am waiting for God to show me the way," when, in reality, we should do as much as we can to make what we want to happen come true. Obviously, we should pray and ask God to help us with everything, but we 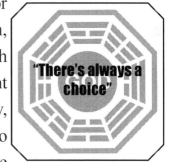 need to do everything we can to help ourselves, and expect God to help us along the way. If He does not, maybe it is not in His will for us to do.

Matthew 28:16-20 talks about the Great Commission. God wants us to go out into the world and spread the gospel. This is not going to happen if we just sit around and do nothing. God told us to work for it. Ephesians 2:10 says, "For we are his workmanship, created in Christ Jesus unto good works, which God hath before ordained that we should walk in them." Colossians 3:23 continues the thought saying, "Whatever you do, work at it with all your heart, as working for the Lord, not for human masters." This tells us to get our motivations straight for what we do. We need to make sure we are doing everything for the glory of God and not men. For if we do things only for applause, then God cannot be happy because we are taking Him out of the equation completely. The emphasis is on doing - action is required.

We should always ask God to guide us and give us direction. Oprah said, "You get in life what you have the courage to ask for." When we feel that God is leading us one way, we need to do all we can to make that objective happen, and trust that God will make it

possible all the way. Even if the feat we are trying to accomplish may seem insurmountable, if it is God's will for us, he will make it possible. "They say the bigger your investment, the bigger your return. But you have to be willing to take a chance. You have to understand, you might lose it all. But if you take that chance, if you invest wisely, the payoff just might surprise you"

(Grey's Anatomy). If it is in His will, then God will allow for it to happen as long as you are willing to do it. We should all have a servant's heart. We all have things that we want to accomplish in life, but what we should really be concerned about is what we think God wants for our life. His wants are important - not ours.

Are you content with your life? Are you in your relationship with Christ?

_____

_____

_____

_____

Do you feel as if you've been going nowhere in your faith and actions?

_____

_____

_____

_____

What is holding you back? Take a moment to pray and ask God for help letting go of these things.

_____
_____
_____
_____

How can you "make your own luck"?

_____
_____
_____
_____

List some names of people who can hold you accountable. Pray for strength to help carry out God's plan for you.

_____
_____
_____
_____

"I'm a great believer in luck, and I find the harder I work the more I have of it."-

–Thomas Jefferson

Chapter 19

■ ■ ■

Locke's Key

Episode 19
"Deus Ex Machina"

In this episode of LOST, Locke faces a myriad of difficult trials. At the beginning, Locke remembers back to his life before the crash, before he is unable to walk. In this flashback, Locke sees a woman following him and confronts her. The woman turns out to be Locke's mother. She claims that Locke does not actually have a father and that he was immaculately conceived.

"You gotta have some faith"

Undeterred by his mother's delusions, Locke goes to a private detective in order to find his father.

As soon as Locke discovers where his father is, he goes to meet him. He and his father go hunting together often and during this time they become very close. Later, when Locke finds out that his father is dying of kidney failure, Locke offers to give one of his kidneys. His father readily accepts the proposal. Locke wakes up from the operation with one less kidney and a missing dad. His mother then reveals to him that his father had just wanted to get in contact with him for the kidney. When he goes back to his dad's house, he is rejected and turned away.

Back on the Island, Locke once again fails to open the hatch; in addition, he also seriously injures his leg and feels no pain. Soon after, he has a strange dream about a plane crashing. In the dream, Boone is chanting a strange phrase and is covered in blood. When he wakes up, Locke takes Boone and the two of them go to find this mysterious plane, hoping to find a way to open the hatch. When they reach their destination, Locke is unable to climb up to the plane and says that Boone has to search it. Boone climbs up to the plane only to discover the dead bodies of heroin smugglers dressed up as priests. He then tries to use the plane's transceiver to call for help, but when doing so, the plane crashes, and Boone suffers serious injuries. Locke carries Boone back to the camp and when Jack asks him what happened, Locke says that Boone fell off of a cliff. Locke quickly leaves the camp and goes to the hatch. The episode ends with Locke pounding on the hatch in anger, crying out about his trials. Just then abrilliant light inside the glass shines out.

Like Locke, who faces trial upon trial in this episode, Joseph in the Bible faced many trials in real life. Joseph is the favorite son of his father, which makes his ten older brothers very jealous. Because of their jealousy, they come up with a plot to get rid of him. In Genesis 37: 27, Joseph is sold as a slave by his brothers and is taken to Egypt where he becomes servant to Potiphar. God stays with Joseph, and because of his loyalty, he is very successful. Joseph soon finds favor with Potiphar and is put in charge of his entire household. Unfortunately, even this successful period of time in his life is short lived. One day when Potiphar is away, his wife tries to seduce Joseph (Genesis 39: 11). When Joseph refuses her, she screams and tells Potiphar that Joseph attacked her. Potiphar believes his wife, and Joseph is thrown in jail. However, the Lord does not leave Joseph, and his faith in God never wavers. In jail, Joseph makes the acquaintance of

Pharaoh's chief baker and chief cupbearer. One night, both of them awake from horrible nightmares and they are very frightened because they do not know what they mean. When they told Joseph about their dreams, with God's help, he was able to interpret them. God told Joseph that in three days, the chief cupbearer would be returned to his post; in the same period of time, the chief baker would be killed. Three days later, Pharaoh gave the chief cupbearer back his job and executed the chief baker.

After two years, Pharaoh has an awful dream and he is unable to determine what it means (Genesis 41:1). He has all of his best dream interpreters come but none of them can figure out its meaning. Only then does the chief cupbearer remember Joseph, and Pharaoh calls upon him to interpret his dream. When Pharaoh tells Joseph his dream, God reveals to Joseph the meaning of the dream: the land of Egypt would have seven years of abundance, followed by seven years of famine. After suggesting a plan to save the food during the time of abundance to use during the famine, Joseph is put in charge of the palace and is made the second most powerful man in Egypt next to Pharaoh. This all happens because he keeps his faith in God and never turns his back on Him. Because of

Joseph, Egypt is prepared for the famine and has plenty of food throughout the seven years of drought.

Joseph is faced with one more challenge when he is reunited with his brothers. The famine has not affected just the Egyptians; Joseph's family has suffered as well. News has spread about how Egypt has a great stockpile of food, and the ten brothers travel there to feed themselves. Upon seeing them, Joseph accuses them of being spies and keeps one brother in Egypt, while the others go back to bring Joseph's other, younger brother. At their return, Joseph holds a feast for his brothers and sends them back. However, he prepares a test for his brothers by leaving a silver cup in the youngest brother's pack to implicate him in a crime.

When the brothers offer themselves in order to save the youngest, Joseph finally reveals his identity and chooses to forgive them for what they had done. He says in Genesis 50:20, "You intended to harm me, but God intended it for good to accomplish what is now being done, the saving of many lives."

In both the episode and in the story of Joseph, characters face many different kinds of trials. Locke has to deal with being manipulated by his father, losing feeling in his legs, and even witnessing Boone's fatal accident. Joseph, on the other hand, is almost killed by his brothers, sold into slavery to Potiphar, and wrongfully placed in prison for something he never did. Needless to say, events spiral out of control, and neither character knows what is in store. As Locke accurately states in the episode, "Our faith is being tested." The same can be true in life; oftentimes trials and tribulations happen seemingly without reason. It often feels like one is being punished unceasingly for nothing at all. Without knowing the end, life can be a confusing mystery.

The most important thing to remember when facing troubles is as Locke says, "You gotta have some faith." Locke stays faithful to his goal of opening the hatch, even when it becomes more and more difficult. Even though his actions seem to yield nothing, he continues pressing onward, no matter how taxing the trials become. The same is true of Joseph. Even though all  of these terrible things happened to him, he remained faithful. When he became a servant to Potiphar, he did the best job that he could. When he was put in prison, he acted with dignity and respect, becoming a leader in prison. Oftentimes, there will be no end in sight and it takes courage in order to remain constant. As Martin Luther King, Jr. once said, "Faith is taking the first step even when you don't see the whole staircase." However, this long-suffering is not in vain, and, as it says in I Peter 1:6-7, "In all this you greatly rejoice, though now for a little while you may have had to suffer grief in all kinds of trials. These have come so that the proven genuineness of your faith—of greater worth than gold, which perishes even though refined by fire—may result in praise, glory and honor when Jesus Christ is revealed."

At the end of trials, there is a wonderful reward. As stated by Charles Spurgeon, "Trials teach us what we are; they dig up the soil, and let us see what we are made of." After the weeks, months, even years of confusion and strife, an end does come. Locke, after struggling through his trials on the Island, finally returns to the hatch, and when he does, the light shines through the window. Joseph also receives a reward in the end, as he becomes second in command in Egypt, and he is reunified with his brothers. Not only are we assured that the pain of trials will come to an eventual end, we are also told that they purify us and make us whole. As stated in James 1:2-4, "Consider it pure joy, my brothers and sisters, whenever you face trials of many kinds, because you know that the testing of your faith produces perseverance. Let perseverance finish its work so that you may be mature and complete, not lacking anything." Ultimately, when faced with trials, the most important part is to stay strong and keep faith. In times of trouble, remember the words of Locke's mother: "You are part of a design." Nothing is meaningless; God has a plan for your trials. It may be difficult, it may be even impossible, but when faced with trials, take heart and know that the end will come. Out of the pain and suffering, something beautiful will emerge.

What trials are you facing right now?

_____

_____

_____

_____

How can God help you stay strong even when your faith is being tested?

_____

_____

_____

_____

Have you overcome any trials in the past? If so, what helped you make it through?

_____

_____

_____

_____

"A gem cannot be polished without friction, nor a man perfected without trials."

–Lucius Annaeus Seneca

Chapter 20

■ ■ ■

Monkey Bars

Episode 20
"Do No Harm"

In this episode of LOST, Boone is seriously injured by falling from a cliff in a wrecked plane that he and Locke discovered. Jack is franticly ordering people around to help with Boone's injuries. Boone's lung collapses and Jack uses a knitting needle to puncture the lung and some tubing to re-inflate it. After this is done, Jack rips open Boone's pants to discover that he has a closed fracture in his leg and begins to set it. This whole time Jack keeps telling Boone that he promises not to let him die and that he's going to make it. While all of this is taking place Kate is off looking for alcohol for Boone's wounds, and she stumbles upon Claire who is having contractions and is in labor. Kate sends Jin to bring Jack so he can deliver the baby;

"I am going to save you"

however, Jin is told that Kate will have to deliver the baby. Meanwhile, nothing that Jack is doing is improving Boone's condition, and his death is imminent. Sun pleads with Jack, asking him to let go and accept that Boone is going to die, but he refuses and decides to amputate Boone's leg because of all the blood that is pooling there. Right before Jack goes through with the amputation, Boone regains consciousness and says, "I know you made a promise. I'm letting you off the hook. Let me go, Jack." Boone dies shortly after. While this is all going on, Kate successfully delivers Claire's baby boy.

God has many ways of testing our faith in Him. One of the ways he does this is by having us "let go" of things in our lives. A very famous instance of this is when God told Abraham to sacrifice Isaac in Genesis 22. God literally said to Abraham, "Take your son, your only son, whom you love—Isaac—and go to the region of Moriah. Sacrifice him there as a burnt offering on a mountain I will show you" (Genesis 22:2). The next day, Abraham gets up, loads up and takes off. On the third day, a day that would become very important in the New Testament, Abraham looks up and sees the mountain on which God specifically told him to sacrifice Isaac. Imagine being Abraham and dreading that moment when the place Isaac would die comes into view. As one can imagine, Isaac is getting suspicious, and he says to his father, "The fire and wood are here, but where is the lamb for the burnt offering?" And Abraham replies, "God himself will provide the lamb for the burnt offering, my son" (Genesis 22:7-8). So they finally reach the mountain and Abraham starts building the altar. When he is finished, he binds his son Isaac. The Bible does not mention a struggle – it seems that Isaac willingly let himself be tied up. Then Abraham lays his son on the altar. Isaac must be terrified in knowing that he is the burnt offering! Now Abraham reaches for the knife, picks it up to slay his son, but 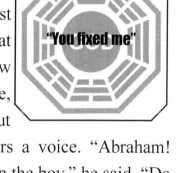 right at that moment, he hears a voice. "Abraham! Abraham! Do not lay a hand on the boy," he said. "Do not do anything to him. Now I know that you fear God, because you have not withheld from me your son, your only son" (Genesis 22:11-12). At this point, Abraham is probably greatly relieved and overjoyed that his son can live, because he proved to be a man who feared God. Then Abraham looks over and sees a ram caught in a bush, for the offering. So Abraham called this place "The Lord Will Provide," and to this day it is said, "On the mountain of the Lord it will be provided" (Genesis 22:14). Then, as a final gift, the angel of the Lord says, "I swear by myself, declares the Lord, that because you have done this and have not withheld your son, your only son, I will surely bless you and make your descendants as numerous as the stars in the sky and as the sand on the seashore. Your descendants will take possession of the cities of their enemies, and through your offspring all nations on earth will be blessed, because you have obeyed me" (Genesis 22:16-18). So really this is a story of letting go, but also one of the provisions and blessings of the Lord, which come to those who fear Him.

When people think of letting go and giving up, it can often be associated with stopping effort or accepting failure. In some situations this may be true, but when God asks us to let go of something, He is not usually telling us to remove our effort. Lao Tzu says, "By letting it go it all gets done. The world is won by those who let it go. But when you try and try. The world is beyond the winning." This connects to

"I will dance at our wedding"

Matthew 6:33, "But seek first his kingdom and his righteousness, and all these things will be given to you as well." When we obey God, He will bless our lives and if we focus on the core of what He is asking, the rest of it will fall into place. When God sets a path for us to follow, He keeps everything in mind and knows how to make it all work out. God understands that we struggle with letting go: whether it is from the memory of a loved one who has died, a past relationship that sticks in our mind, or a sin that we cannot seem to give up on. Jack and Abraham represent two very opposite examples of how people struggle with letting go. Jack was fighting it until the end, and he really was adding harm to the situation by trying too hard to save Boone. He gave so much of his own blood that he could no longer think straight or make good decisions. Jack's father tells him as he is trying to write his own wedding vows that, "it's commitment that makes you tick," which for him, answered whether marriage was the right thing. Yet, in this situation, as soon as he made the promise to save Boone's life, he was committed to accomplishing that. He could not give up on his word, and was so committed that he was willing to do whatever it took.

On the other hand, Abraham was so faithful to God that he would do anything he was asked, even give up his own son. In Proverbs 3:5-6 it says, "Trust in the LORD with all your heart and lean not on your own understanding; in all your ways acknowledge him, and he will make your paths straight." God explains how He is in control and that obeying Him will make everything all right. Abraham takes this to heart and is willing to accept that God has the best in mind for him and his son. For Abraham, instead of worrying about keeping his promise to God, it was scarier how easily he was willing to part with his only child based on his faith. Instead of just giving up when he was asked to let go of his son, Abraham put more effort than before just to keep his promise. That is what God asks from each of us: to be willing to let go of anything He tells us to, and put more effort into keeping that promise then it takes to hold onto something.

Leo Buscaglia says, "Let go. Why do you cling to pain? There is nothing you can do about the wrongs of yesterday. It is not yours to judge. Why hold on to the very thing which keeps you from hope and love?". Even though we cannot always see God's plan for our lives, He has the best end result for each of us in mind. It is very important that we constantly remind ourselves that He knows infinitely more than us about ourselves and that when we obey Him when He tells us to let go of what we hold onto so dearly. Even when it seems that what we hold onto is making us better, God ultimately knows whether or not it is negatively affecting our lives, and more importantly, hurting our relationship with Him. Let's let go and let God.

Have you ever struggled with letting go of the memory of someone, either a past relationship that you couldn't get over, or a close friend or family member who died? Who did you turn to in your struggle? Was your struggle ever relieved?

_____

_____

_____

_____

Have you ever seen a friend struggle with letting go of someone or something? Were you there to help him? Did he express his struggles to you? How did he overcome his struggles/does he still struggle with letting go?

_____

_____

_____

_____

Do you feel like God is asking you to let go of something right now? If YES, are you willing to obey him? Do you know why He is asking you to let go? If NO, have you ever felt God asking you to let go in the past? How difficult was it to obey Him?

_____

_____

_____

_____

What was/is a temptation that you struggled/struggle with? If you have let it go, does it still tempt you at times? Have you encountered new temptations since you let the old one(s) go? Have they been easy to deal with now that you have overcome temptation before?

_____

_____

_____

_____

"**The only way to make sense out of change is to plunge into it, move with it, and join the dance.**"

–Alan Watts

Chapter 21

■ ■ ■

Hit the Pause Button

Episode 21
"The Greater Good"

After a series of catastrophic events, specifically Boone's death, everyone's nerves are on edge. When Locke returns, he is met with hostility and aggression for leaving without an explanation. Instead of taking the time to listen to what Locke has to say, Jack attacks him in a fury. Sayid is having issues of his own as flashbacks of his old friend Essam plague his mind.

In an undercover attempt to retrieve stolen explosives for the CIA, he is forced to persuade his friend to be a suicide bomber, only to reveal the truth at the last possible second. Terribly hurt, Essam acts in a moment of extreme passion and takes his own life. Sayid, remembering this pain, tries to console Shannon, only to watch her slip deeper into grief. Shannon, the most affected by Boone's death, acts on impulse and stalks down Locke in the jungle with a gun she stole from Jack. Luckily, Jack, Kate, and Sayid realize the gun is missing and confront Shannon before she can pull the trigger.

"Baby Huey is like nails on a chalkboard"

Adam and Eve bore two sons: Cain, the first born, and Abel, the second. Cain became a farmer who worked the soil and Abel kept the flocks. One day, Cain and Abel brought two offerings to the Lord. "The Lord looked with favor on Abel and his offering, but on Cain and his offering he did not look with favor. So Cain was very angry and his face was downcast" (Genesis 4:4-5). "Then the Lord said to Cain, "Why are you angry? Why is your face downcast? If you do what is right, will you not be accepted? But if you do not do what is right, sin is crouching at your door; it desires to have you, but you must rule over it" (Genesis 4:6-7). The Lord tries to give Cain a pep talk by telling him that he must rule over his selfish and sinful desires. The pep talk the Lord gave Cain did not work; he was still flustered. As a result of his anger, Cain tricks Abel to go to the field, and kills him.

"So much for my philosophy degree"

Have you ever felt so angry that you wanted to deal with it in an irrational way? Shannon experienced this situation through her anger that she held toward Locke. Her idea of dealing with the situation was to kill Locke in cold blood, which was quite familiar to that of Cain and Abel. Ephesians 4:26-27 says, "Be angry and do not sin; do not let the sun go down on your anger, and give no opportunity to the devil." Shannon is in the wrong because she has given an opportunity to the devil. The devil wanted to use her to take revenge on a man who is more than likely innocent. Her anger blinded her from seeing the whole situation clearly allowing for the devil to take control and do what he wants.

Donald Calne, Director of the Neurodegenerative Disorders Centre at the University of British Columbia and a professor of neurology says, "The essential difference between emotion and reason is that emotion leads to action while reason leads to conclusion."

Emotion and reason are both necessary to make a good choice according to his definition. The anger Shannon holds inside causes her reasons to be blinded. The same thing happens to Cain when he plots to kill Abel. Aristotle wrote, "Anybody can become angry - that is easy, but to be angry with the right person and to the right degree and at the right time and for the right purpose, and in the right way - that is not within everybody's power and is not easy." Aristotle states that it is not easy to be angry for the right reasons. However, to control one's emotions is not an impossible task.

When someone cannot control his own emotions, he can be led down a path of wickedness. Shannon and Cain were following the wrong path that was filled with wickedness. Cain chose not to control his anger towards Abel, and as a result, Cain killed Abel. Shannon possessed the same anger that grew within Cain, the anger that blinds people from making the right choices. However, Shannon learns to control her anger with the help of her friends. They persuade her not to kill Locke, because if she does she will ultimately find out that he was innocent, causing her to regret her decision. Anger clouds people's judgment just like it did to both Cain and Shannon. In conclusion, people should take precautions and learn self-control in order to control their emotions. Emotions can turn someone into what he does not want to be. He ends up not doing what is pleasing to God and following His path of righteousness. Proverbs 29:11 states, "A fool gives full vent to his anger, but a wise man keeps him under control."

What are some ways that you can develop self-control?

_____

_____

_____

_____

Have you ever experienced anger similar to Shannon and Cain?

_____

_____

_____

_____

What are some things that have triggered your emotions? Why?

_____

_____

_____

_____

"Any emotion, if it is sincere, is involuntary."
–Mark Twain

Chapter 22

■ ■ ■

Rep Rap

Episode 22
"Born to Run"

"I'm a doctor, you're a hillbilly"

Have you ever done something or said something in order to keep a good reputation? Even if that meant you had to lie in order to have that good reputation. In Episode 22, we see several people concerned for their reputation. Kate is concerned that her past will be revealed, hurting her reputation, and Walt is concerned that his actions of burning the boat will hurt his reputation. Both Walt and Kate had to make decisions, either lie or tell the truth in order to try to keep their good reputation. There is a similar story in the Bible to this idea of a good and bad reputation in 1 Samuel 15-

20 which starts with a conversation between God and Samuel. God told Samuel, "I am grieved that I have made Saul king because he has turned away from me and has not carried out my instructions." Later on Saul came to Samuel saying, "The Lord bless you! I have carried out the Lord's instructions." But then Samuel had to reveal to Saul what the Lord told him the night before. Saul had not obeyed the Lord and plundered his enemy. Saul's excuse for the plunder of the enemy's animals was so they could make sacrifices to the Lord. Samuel then explained: "Does the Lord delight in burnt offerings and sacrifices as much as in obeying

"It was something in the water"

the voice of the Lord? To obey is better than sacrifice." Since Saul rejected the word of the Lord, the Lord rejected him as king. The Lord took the kingdom of Israel from Saul and gave it to one of his neighbors. Then, until the day Samuel died, he did not see Saul again but mourned for him. Once again the Lord was grieved that he had made Saul the king over Israel.

In this episode of LOST, Kate is revealed to be the criminal, and her reputation on the Island is severely dampened. After Sawyer tells everyone the truth, Kate just wants to continue helping, in order regain the previous flawless reputation. Despite her trying to hide her past, it is still revealed. Then there is Walt who his hiding the secret of burning the first raft. Although he knows he could just turn away and never tell his dad, he wants to. He wants his dad to trust him. This means telling him the truth, no matter how difficult.

Wayne W. Dyer once said, "Your reputation is in the hands of others. That's what the reputation is. You can't control that. The only thing you can control is your character." This quote applies to Kate and Sawyer. Sawyer spilled the beans on Kate. He let everyone know about her past, letting them know that she was the criminal who was on the flight. Sawyer saying this about Kate, ruined her reputation with many of the people on the Island. They no longer saw her as helpful, but as dangerous. This is where 2 Peter 2:12 comes in.

"Track 2: Monster eats the pilot"

2 Peter 2:12 says, "Live such good lives among the pagans that, though they accuse you of doing wrong, they may see your good deeds and glorify God on the day he visits us." God commands us as Christians to act a certain way. When we do not act in that way, the devil

starts to creep in, and our walk will be challenged by others. If Kate had been upfront with everybody then perhaps they wouldn't have been as frightened about her being bad.

Another quote that fits this episode and idea of reputations is from Israelmore Ayivor: "It's easier to maintain a good character than to recover it when it's gone bad!" Walt messed up. He burned the raft, and Locke knew about it. When his dad was poisoned, he wanted to make sure that Locke knew that he did not poison his dad. He wanted to make sure his character was clean with Locke. He also came clean with his dad about burning the first raft. By doing this, he showed that he trusted his dad and wanted to make sure he was on good terms with him. As Christians, we need to be in constant check of our character. Once a reputation gets spotted, even just a little bit, a person loses some of his authority. We need to always be seeking forgiveness and forgiving others in order to maintain a good and respectable reputation.

Acts 24:16 says, "So I strive always to keep my conscience clear before God and man." It is important to remember we need to be honest with everyone. When Walt tells his dad how he burned the raft, it wasn't going to change their current future but it was important for his dad to know he is sorry. Another point the verse connects with is the fact that we should keep the conscience clear – no one else should reveal our past. If we keep a clear conscience then we can hold up a good reputation, built on trust and honesty; whether it be to God or our peers.

Do you strive to have a good reputation?

_____
_____
_____
_____

Are you hiding something that could ruin your reputation?

_____
_____
_____
_____

Do you think it is easier for someone to announce your mistake or for you to tell them? Regardless of which is easier, which is better?

_____

_____

_____

_____

Do you think how your actions will affect your reputations before you go through with them?

_____

_____

_____

_____

Do you worry more about your reputations with your peers, or with God?

_____

_____

_____

_____

"It takes many good deeds to build a good reputation, and only one bad one to lose it."

— Benjamin Franklin

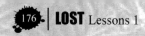

Chapter 23

■ ■ ■

Hiding in a Hatch of Sin

Episode 23
"Exodus (Part 1)"

Episode 23 starts off with Walt discovering Rousseau, the French women. Rousseau tells the story of how she was shipwrecked 16 years ago. When she landed on the Island, she was with six other people, and she was already seven months pregnant. She delivered the baby herself; however the black smoke came and took her baby. Rousseau tells them the black smoke is now coming for them. Later, Jack is concerned that Rousseau is crazy and will ruin the raft launch. But Locke  suggests that they should focus on launching the raft anyway. When they finally do decide to launch the raft, it slips off the rails and severely damages the raft. Later Jack devises a plan to open the hatch with explosives and explains that they have to go back to Rousseau's base to acquire them. Jack explains to everyone that they need to open the hatch in order to hide from the black smoke and the others about how Rousseau warned them. Everyone then starts to say their goodbyes to the people leaving on the raft, and Walt decides to give Vincent to Shannon.

In this episode of LOST, everyone starts to hear about "The Others" and they decide to try opening the hatch and hide in it.. In the Bible, many people in the Old Testament hid from what they had done. In Genesis, Adam and Eve were the first people created and were given one rule, not to eat of the tree of knowledge of good and evil. While Eve was in the garden she was

"Nitroglycerin is extremely temperamental."

tempted by Satan, at the time being in form of a serpent, to eat of the fruit that the tree produced. Eve ate of the fruit and then told Adam to eat of it. After knowing that they had sinned, they hid from God and from their sin. Afterwards, God called them out, and they were banished from the Garden. Do not be like

Adam and Eve and hide from your sin, but confront it. If you hide from your sin, it will eat away at you and cause you pain.

I'm sure you have heard of the saying, "Whatever happens in Vegas stays in Vegas." Well that is just false advertising. Proverb 15:3 says, "The eyes of LORD are in every place, beholding the evil and the good." God sees whatever you are doing in your daily life. Number 32:23 says, "But if you will not do so, behold, you have sinned against the LORD: and be sure your sin will find you out." Most people misinterpret this verse as, "Your sins will one day be exposed." But what Moses really meant is that the sin we committed will one day come back and haunt us. The world is a sinful place. Every single one of us has sinned. In fact, as you get closer to God, you will realize you are the biggest sinner of all because God's holiness exposes our wickedness. James 2:10 tells us that breaking one of the commandments is equivalent to breaking all of them from God's point of view. So are we supposed to give up trying just because we sinned once? No, we need to confess our sins and accept Christ as our savior. God sent his only child,

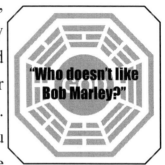

"Who doesn't like Bob Marley?"

Jesus, to die so His blood could wash away our sins. Even the great Apostle Paul had sinned and asked to be saved. He says in 1 Timothy 1:15, "This is a faithful saying, and worthy of all acceptation: that Christ Jesus came into the world to save sinners, for whom I am chief." We need to recognize our sins and allow the blood of Jesus to wash away our sins so we can be saved and spend eternity with our God in heaven.

Nelson Mandela understood struggles as he said, "I am not a saint, unless you think of a saint as a sinner who keeps on trying." Perfection doesn't come until Heaven. We will sin, but we can't just run and hide. We need to keep on trying to do what is right.

How do you hide from your sin?

_____

_____

_____

_____

How do you hide from your sin?

_____

_____

_____

_____

How do you hide from your sin?

_____

_____

_____

_____

Do you find yourself hiding from your sin often? How do you think you can fix this?

_____

_____

_____

_____

"The worst sin towards our fellow creatures is to be dishonest
with them and not reveal our essence of humanity."

— George Bernard Shaw

Chapter 24

■ ■ ■

Diving into Destiny

Episode 24
"Exodus (Part 2)"

Episode 24 focuses on destiny; Jack tries to control his destiny tricking Kate and carrying the highly volatile dynamite. Rousseau emphasizes the effect of the past on the future by warning the flight survivors about the impending doom surrounding the black smoke in the distance. "Exodus" is also an episode of hope as Walt, Jin, Sawyer and Michael are finally ready to leave on their makeshift raft, along with their journey comes an expectation of rescue and they must put aside their differences and work together to fulfill what they believe to be their fate and best chance of getting saved.

At a pivotal point of the episode, Locke says, "We were all brought to this Island for a purpose!" Sometimes we don't realize God is working behind the scenes to actually place us where He wants. In the Bible, Jonah was told by God to go to the city of Nineveh. This city was known for their sinful nature and complete disregard

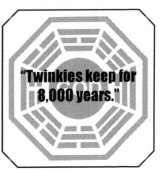

"Twinkies keep for 8,000 years."

for God. Jonah was afraid to go to Nineveh so he tried to run and hide from God and headed towards Tarshish instead. The sailors of this ship who took him towards Tarshish were nervous because of the fierce storm that came upon them. Jonah explained to the crew that it was his fault the storm was upon them, that he was running from God. The sailors threw him overboard and the storm stopped instantly. Meanwhile, a big fish sent from God swallowed up Jonah. "And the LORD appointed a great fish to swallow Jonah, and Jonah was in the stomach of the fish three days and three nights" (Jonah 1:17). After three days the fish coughed Jonah up as God had commanded it to do. Jonah then obeyed God and headed to Nineveh. When he arrived at Nineveh, he preached to the Ninevites to repent, and he was surprised as the sinful city repented before God. "Then the people of Nineveh believed in God; and they called a fast and put on sackcloth from the greatest to the least of them" (Jonah 3:5). God taught Jonah of His love and mercy and showed him everything He does is for a purpose. "... I knew that You are a gracious and compassionate God, slow to anger and abundant in loving kindness, and one who relents concerning calamity" (Jonah 4:2)

Jin, Michael, Sawyer, and Walt all get on the boat they built to escape the Island to find rescue, because they believe that is what is best for them. Jonah ran away from God because he did not want to go to Nineveh; he believed it was best for him to run away. These are two different situations, but they share a common theme. Although the men and Jonah believe they know what they are doing, and that they are doing what is best for them, they both end in unfortunate ways.

"You got some Arzt on you."

Because Michael thinks leaving is the best thing for him and his son, he loses Walt to the strangers on the fishing boat. Because Jonah thought he knew what was best for him and ran away, a fish came and ate him up, and spat him out at Nineveh. These two different situations can relate to our lives when we question our purpose or think we know what is best for ourselves when really, it's not what's best.

To those who are struggling to find their purpose in life, just know you do have a purpose. We are all here for a specific reason to do a specific part in furthering the mission of God. John F. Kennedy once said, "Efforts and courage are not enough without purpose and direction." There is not another person out there like you - we all have different and unique purposes that in the end all come down to the same thing, and that's furthering the Mission.

What things distract you from finding or fulfilling your purpose?

_____

_____

_____

_____

Our purpose comes from God. The reason we live in a certain place, do a certain task, is all because of that purpose. Unfortunately, sometimes we let ourselves get in the way of that purpose. Jonah did not want to fulfill the task God had instructed him to do, and ran away. Although he may have thought that was the end of that, God had other plans. He went as far as getting a fish to swallow Jonah up and make him realize he had to go to Nineveh. When we feel like we have it all under control and don't need anyone, or we know what we are supposed to do but choose not to do it, God will find a way to bring us back to that purpose whether we like it or not.

Hurley was going to miss his flight in this episode. Even though he was late, he still "luckily" found a way onto the plane. Had he taken the next flight, he might have never crashed on the Island; but, what if Hurley was never on the Island? Would his contribution be missing and make the others have a harder time surviving? Each person on that Island contributes in some way to help everyone survive. Jack is the doctor, Sayid is the  technician - they each have a different purpose; if one was gone from the Island, a piece to survival would be missing. Thomas Merton said, "If you want to identify me, ask me not where I live, or what I like to eat, or how I comb my hair, but ask me what I am living for, in detail, ask me what I think is keeping me from living fully for the thing I want to live for." We need to identify our mission and stay true to it.

What things do you hold on to that distract you from your purpose?

_____

_____

_____

_____

What do you think God's purpose for you is?

_____

_____

_____

_____

What gifts or talents do you contribute to this "Island?"

_____

_____

_____

_____

To what "city" are you running to avoid going to Nineveh?

_____

_____

_____

_____

To what "city" are you running to avoid going to Nineveh?

_____

_____

_____

_____

"The only reason for time is so everything doesn't happen at once."
— Albert Einstein

Conclusion: ONE WAY

After faithfully following and watching LOST for 6 seasons, it ended, as one would expect from Hollywood. The authors, Randy Johnson and David Rutledge, would like to make a final observation and clarification.

LOST closes with everyone entering the front door of the church, except Jack who gets in "through the back door." It is subtle, but a statement is being made that there are many ways to Heaven. As he enters the room, this idea is enforced, as religious symbols of Judaism, Islam, Buddhism, Hinduism, Taoism and New Age Spirituality are displayed. The writers of LOST like to make a point without saying a word. In this back entry, it is realized that all roads (beliefs and religions) lead to the same place.

Christianity does not accept this Universalism. The Bible is clear that there is only way to Heaven and that is through Jesus Christ. John 14:6 says, "Jesus answered, 'I am the way and the truth and the life. No one comes to the Father except through me.'" Jesus is not just a way; He is the way to Heaven. This verse leaves no room for hidden passageways. Acts 4:12 continues the thought and says, "Salvation is found in no one else, for there is no other name under heaven given to men by which we must be saved." The context is referring to Jesus. He is the only way to salvation.

Christianity is unique from all other religions. When others are striving to get to God, Christianity is based on God coming to man. When others are stressing sacrificing and dying for God, Christianity emphasizes the sacrifice and death of God for man. Christianity focuses on Christ, while all other religions focus on man.

One final thought: If there were other ways to Heaven, why would God let Jesus die? If there are other ways to Heaven, then God is either dumb or very unloving to have let His only Son die on the cross. Jesus is the ONE WAY.

"There is a God shaped vacuum in the heart of every man which cannot be filled by any created thing, but only by God, the Creator, made known through Jesus."
–Blaise Pascal

About the Authors

Dr. Randy Johnson has been married to Angela for over 30 years. They have two children, Clint and Stephanie. He has been Chaplain and Bible teacher at Oakland Christian School for over 20 years. He also ministers at two local Chinese Church youth groups. He wrote And Then Some, LOST Lessons, Little While Times, Dream in English and created Read316.com.

Dr. David Rutledge has been working in youth ministry for over 15 years as a Bible teacher, a youth pastor and a speaker. David has a degree in Biblical Studies/Christian Education of Youth and History from Cedarville University, a Masters of Education from Regent University and a Doctorate of Education from Liberty University. David lives with his wife Rebekah and children in Burbank California. He also wrote LOST Lessons.

To order additional copies of **LOST** Lessons 1 or
to find out more by Dr. Randy Johnson,
David Rutledge or other life changing books
published by Rochester Media,
please visit our website **www.rochestermedia.com**

Discounts are available for ministry and
retail purposes.

Contact Rochester Media

Rochester Media LLC
P.O. Box 80002
Rochester, MI 48308
248-429-READ
info@rochestermedia.com

Made in the USA
San Bernardino, CA
14 May 2014